PLAYS FROM VAULT

EGGS
Florence Keith-Roach

MR INCREDIBLE
Camilla Whitehill

PRIMADONNA
Rosie Kellett

CORNERMEN
Oli Forsyth

RUN
Stephen Laughton

PLAYS FROM VAULT

EGGS
Florence Keith-Roach

MR INCREDIBLE
Camilla Whitehill

PRIMADONNA
Rosie Kellett

CORNERMEN
Oli Forsyth

RUN
Stephen Laughton

NICK HERN BOOKS
London
www.nickhernbooks.co.uk

A Nick Hern Book

Plays from VAULT first published in Great Britain in 2016 as a paperback original by Nick Hern Books Limited, The Glasshouse, 49a Goldhawk Road, London W12 8QP, in association with VAULT Festival

Cover image: Thomas K Shannon

Designed and typeset by Nick Hern Books, London
Printed and bound in Great Britain by Mimeo Ltd, Huntingdon, Cambridgeshire PE29 6XX

A CIP catalogue record for this book is available from the British Library

ISBN 978 1 84842 553 8

Contents

Welcome to VAULT

For six weeks in bleakest winter, VAULT Festival transforms the dark tunnels underneath Waterloo Station into a carnival of experiences, every nook and cranny filled with entertainment and around every corner an unexpected adventure.

VAULT is a place to discuss, and a place to party: every night you can join hundreds of artists and explorers for gigs, parties and performances. Since 2012, we have hosted over 250 productions from Britain's most exciting emerging artists.

We're trying to reinvent the business model of the non-funded creative sector and make it sustainable for both the artist and the festival. We can't offer luxury, but what we can give is space: to innovate, take risks and collaborate with each other without the huge financial burdens you'll find across the Thames, and in big institutions.

We're delighted to present this collection of new writing. Though not everything at VAULT starts (or even ends) with a script, we hope you'll find these five plays to be a cross-section of the exciting new talent which courses through the Festival's veins.

Andy George, Mat Burt, and Tim Wilson
VAULT Festival Directors

This book went to press before the end of rehearsals and so the texts may differ slightly from the plays as performed.

EGGS

Florence Keith-Roach

For Lily

Florence Keith-Roach is a writer, actor and director working across theatre, television and film, who has been named a 'rising star of the London theatre scene' (*Evening Standard*).

Her debut play, *Love To Love To Love You*, which she wrote, directed and acted in, transferred to VAULT Festival in 2015 where it sold out, and was named one of *Another Magazine*'s 'top ten things to do'. A work-in-progress version of her second play, *Eggs*, opened at the Edinburgh Free Fringe in August 2015. It received five-star reviews and was described as 'Honest. Human. Real. Frank. Funny. Achingly relevant' by *Broadway Baby*. She has written for *Grazia*, the *Observer* and *Little White Lies* about her experiences as a writer, director and actor in both film and theatre. She is the founder of Orphee Productions, a female-led collective dedicated to telling stories that challenge gender preconceptions. Her short film, *Frenching the Bully*, which she co-wrote, directed and acted with Freddy Syborn is available to watch online. She has a lead role in the feature film, *Here Lies*, which was awarded the Best European Independent Feature Film of 2015.

2

Acknowledgements

With very special thanks to Maud Dromgoole; dramaturg and director of *Eggs* in Edinburgh.

Eternal gratitude to Michal Murawski, the ultimate polo-necked pundit, Wendy and Stephen Keith-Roach, Christine Bramwell, Imy Wyatt-Corner, Stuart Snaith, Charlie Hanson, Eloise Lawson, Imogen Lloyd, Zander Levy, Emily Bartelott, Coral Amiga, Tor Lupton, Harriet Green, Lauren Cooney, James Lambert, the Cheetham family, Chiara Goldsmith, George Belfield & Sex Club (may this stand as an homage to our symposia!).

F. K-R.

Eggs was first performed at VAULT Festival, London, on 24 February 2016, with the following cast:

GIRL ONE	Florence Keith-Roach
GIRL TWO	Amani Zardoe

Producer	Lucie Massey
Set Designer	Clementine Keith-Roach
Costume Designer	Lily Ashley
Associate Producer	Hannah Tookey
Executive Producer	Alex Timken
Lighting Designer	Lucy Hansom
Sound Designer	Jon McLeod
Poster Designer	Clementine Keith-Roach
Photography	Lily Ashley

Eggs is brought to you by Orphee Productions, a female-led collective dedicated to telling stories which challenge gender disparity.

A work-in-progress version of *Eggs* premiered at the Edinburgh Free Fringe 2015.

Characters

GIRL ONE
GIRL TWO

A dash (–) indicates the next line interrupts.

A forward slash (/) indicates an overlap.

Scene One

A hospital. March. 2016. The end.

GIRL ONE. It's not just the eggs themselves, it's the hypocrisy of the vegetarians who eat them.

GIRL TWO. What else have they got to eat?

GIRL ONE. It's really weird, think about it?

GIRL TWO. No actually, can you stop. I don't want to think about eggs any more, thank you.

GIRL ONE. Okay, okay, so I was at a café the other day with *Save-the-world Suki* and she spent, ah so long, tut, tut, tutting up and down the menu, whinging that it wasn't 'veggie friendly', whatever that means? Only to shut up, finally, and agree to have a Spanish omelette. Now, I didn't think anything of it either, at first, I was just thinking how absurd Suki has gotten –

GIRL TWO. Yeah, she really has, why did you –

GIRL ONE. But the next morning, I found myself cracking an egg for my dad, like the 1950s house-slave that I am –

GIRL TWO. Ha, that's what you get for still living at home –

GIRL ONE. And I looked into this orange orb floating in a glistening, gooey, well, placenta –

GIRL TWO. Ahhhhhhh –

GIRL ONE. And it hit me. WOW. This is an unborn chicken. This is so much an unborn chicken that it is almost grossing ME out and I am a proper carnivore. I'm, like, the first to be mouth-deep in some still-beating blood and muscle. But even I can see that there is something really dark about eating an unborn child.

GIRL TWO. You're chatting shit, complete unscientific shit. An egg is not an embryo, it's not yet fertilised.

GIRL ONE. Oh, come on? I am not talking scientifically, I am talking emotionally! Like, it's just as bad as eating a normal adult animal. Way worse even. Cos your average mature pig has probably led, in animal years and as long as you don't get any of that factory-farmed stuff, a pretty long and happy life. You know, in the bosom of her loving, surprisingly hygienic family, a little hut to rest her snout in, the gentle hum of the A303 rolling by. Charming. Whereas, here, here is this aborted thing, this thing with the promise of a life filled with fields and feed, ripped from its mother's downy breast and shoved into a cardboard box to be devoured by the pointed incisors of holier-than-thou hypocrites!

Pause.

Sorry, I didn't mean to go on about its unfulfilled life or anything. That wasn't very… Considering you just… I'm not against abortions at all. Just vegetarians eating eggs.

Pause.

Sound and light fill the stage.

Scene Two

A landing. January. 2015. The beginning.

A doorbell rings.

GIRL ONE *rushes to the door, she doesn't open it but talks from behind it, clearly disturbed.*

GIRL ONE. What took you so long?

GIRL TWO. What do you mean? I ran all the way.

GIRL ONE. Did you bring the razor?

GIRL TWO. Yes, but… What is going on?

GIRL ONE. Okay, so if you could just slide it through the letter box and leave, that would be great.

GIRL TWO. What? No, not if you are going to cut your wrists with it.

GIRL ONE. Just slide it and leave. Thank you.

GIRL TWO. I am not a delivery service.

GIRL ONE. You only live two streets away.

GIRL TWO. That's not the point. Come on, let me in.

GIRL ONE. That's not a good idea.

GIRL TWO. Why not? What is going on? This is fucking out of order.

She bangs on the door.

GIRL ONE. No, shhh. You'll wake the neighbours.

GIRL TWO. They're all still out partying.

GIRL ONE. It's for your own good.

GIRL TWO. Listen to me. It is okay. It is all going to be okay.

GIRL ONE. Go home and do some work. You know you want to.

GIRL TWO. Open the door. Open the DOOOORRRRRRRRR!

She starts banging on the door, screaming.

Eventually, GIRL ONE *opens the door, she has wet hair and red eyes.*

Oh my god, you've gelled your hair!

GIRL ONE. What? No. I've got nits!

GIRL TWO (*jumping back*). Err. Really? Rank.

GIRL ONE. I know. So just give me the razor and go away, before it's too late.

GIRL TWO. It is 7 a.m. on New Year's Day. I thought you were going to kill yourself!

GIRL ONE. Oh chill out. It's not like you weren't tucked up in bed with Miss Marple by 10 p.m.?

GIRL TWO. That's not the point. And I wasn't.

This is so fucking typical of you! You selfish. You selfish… dunt!

GIRL ONE. Dunt?

GIRL TWO. Who do you think you are?

GIRL ONE. Please. Just give me the razor.

GIRL TWO. You don't need a razor, you need a nit comb.

GIRL ONE. I've got a nit comb. A fucking expensive nit comb. The woman in the chemist royally ripped me off. She kept asking how old my infected child was. The bitch.

GIRL TWO. I mean it's a fairly logical question, it is pretty rare for anyone over twelve to have nits.

GIRL ONE. No, she knows I don't have a child. I mean, I was in there, like, every weekend last year to get the free morning-after pill. We've discussed, at length, how irresponsible and un-maternal I am. Not to mention how barren I probably am, which admittedly made the whole pill thing a bit of a charade, but it's free, so… No, she was just trying to fluster me so that I'd go for the TURBO comb. Twice as expensive.

GIRL TWO. Well maybe TURBO is a good thing?

GIRL ONE. It hasn't worked. I have been up all night scraping my scalp raw and the population is not dwindling. I even tried to nuke the fuckers, I submerged my head in a bath of vodka, you know, to make them drunk and defenceless? I mean if it worked with the Native Americans? But no joy.

GIRL TWO. How do you always manage to make a reference to your colonialism essay?

GIRL ONE. It was a great essay, only three per cent of our year got a first, and you weren't one of them –

GIRL TWO. That was five years ago. Get over it. You are so deranged.

GIRL ONE. Well you'd feel deranged too if your boyfriend had squealed in disgust when he saw a nit jump from your head. As you were giving him head.

GIRL TWO. What? There is no way he could have seen that. Anyway, he is not your boyfriend.

GIRL ONE. We've been together for four months.

GIRL TWO. But you've only seen each other, like, four times.

GIRL ONE. It's the quality not the quantity. God you always demean my relationships.

GIRL TWO. No, I am just protective. He ditches you after sex every time.

GIRL ONE. He's Swiss, he can't handle fraught emotions.

GIRL TWO. So, he's pathetic as well as a dick?

GIRL ONE. He saw a nit jump from my head to his pubic hair. How was he supposed to react?

GIRL TWO. How did he even see it?

GIRL ONE. He wears very thick glasses and it was a big one. Like a prawn. He said I was a rancid nest of bad hygiene and then he left.

GIRL TWO. I mean?

GIRL ONE (*hiccuping*). It was so sad cos it was the first time I have ever spent New Year's Eve with a boyfriend, it was going to be a really great date –

GIRL TWO. What? Where he'd come round, get head and leave? –

GIRL ONE. And instead I was left downing two bottles of prosecco with a bleeding scalp.

GIRL TWO (*suppressing laughter*). But where on earth did you get nits from?

GIRL ONE. He said I got them from the dogs.

GIRL TWO. Dogs have fleas not nits.

GIRL ONE. Yeah, but he said they can, like, transmute on human blood.

GIRL TWO. Ah, so he's an idiot as well as a dick.

GIRL ONE. Well it does make sense. I am walking them day in day out.

GIRL TWO. But –

GIRL ONE. Ah, it's so rank when you get, like, a row of eggs on the comb. Like, fish-egg roe. Growing on my scalp.

GIRL TWO. Stop it.

GIRL ONE. I think, like, the plethora of fertile eggs breeding on my head, is particularly abrasive to my sensibility because, you know, I am a product of IVF. It –

GIRL TWO. You refer everything to IVF. It's so irrelevant.

GIRL ONE. Not to me and the thousands of other, poor, synthetic children it isn't.

Pause.

GIRL TWO. So why do you want the razor? You are going to kill yourself, aren't you?

GIRL ONE. No. I am going to shave my hair off.

GIRL TWO. What? No you can't. You'll look terrible.

GIRL ONE. No I won't. I'll look like Natalie Portman.

GIRL TWO. You haven't got her bone structure. You have a massive forehead. You will look like an egg. A nit egg.

GIRL ONE. Or Sinéad O'Connor? Please, I am going to tear my skin off.

GIRL TWO. No one will employ you –

GIRL ONE. As a dog-walker? No one gives a shit.

GIRL TWO. You'll never get asked out.

GIRL ONE. Oh no! Like, that's the worst thing you can imagine.

GIRL TWO. You'll never get your boyfriend back. Or… get to give him head.

GIRL ONE. God, you are such a square.

GIRL TWO. Oh and you are so hard? Miss 'I Was Raised in a Barn'.

GIRL ONE. Um, it was a renovated coach house.

GIRL TWO. Jesus. First the tattoo and now you're shaving your head?

GIRL ONE. The tattoo? The tattoo is totally unrelated, why are you bringing that up?

GIRL TWO. What are you trying to prove?

GIRL ONE. Nothing. I just –

GIRL TWO. Whatever, you just better not ring me up at 3 a.m. again crying about how much you, 'hate your egg head', because this square is not interested.

GIRL ONE. That never happened. I do not hate my tattoo.

GIRL TWO. Yes you do. You said it looks like a 'giant brussel sprout'.

GIRL ONE. It's a wild rose. There is just quite a lot of foliage around it.

GIRL TWO. 'A giant brussel sprout', growing out of your bum crack.

GIRL ONE. Well it's in memory of my dead best friend, so fuck you.

Pause.

GIRL TWO. Rose was my friend too.

Pause.

You're right, you would look good with a shaved head. Very *This is England*.

GIRL ONE. Sinéad O'Connor is fine by me. Give me the razor, please.

GIRL TWO *holds up her disposable razor.*

GIRL TWO (*brandishing the razor*). Why don't I do it for you? You'll never reach those back bits alone and we wouldn't want it to look patchy.

GIRL ONE. No thanks, I'd rather do it myself. You know, mourn the loss of these golden tresses in private.

GIRL TWO. Ginger tresses. Go on, sit down. I'll be neat.

GIRL ONE. Um, no thanks, just give me the razor.

GIRL TWO. Got any shaving foam?

GIRL ONE. Alright, creepy.

GIRL TWO. Not chickening out are you? Triangle?

GIRL ONE. Is this about me calling you a square? You have got to be less sensitive.

GIRL TWO. Come on, sit.

GIRL ONE. I was actually planning on more of an undercut thing… it's quite niche –

GIRL TWO. Sit in the chair.

GIRL ONE. Leave me alone. Okay? I've had a long night, I'm emotionally frazzled, I'm still drunk, I'm having an episode –

GIRL TWO. Sit in the fucking chair.

She sits. GIRL TWO *approaches. Menacing.*

(*Singing.*) Nothing compares, nothing compares, to you.

Sound and light fill the stage.

Scene Three

A park. March. 2015.

GIRL TWO *is power-walking on the spot for most of their interaction.*

GIRL ONE *occasionally attempts to join in, but spends most of the scene stationary, crossing and uncrossing her legs.*

A little buzz can be faintly heard.

GIRL TWO. You look cheery.

GIRL ONE *giggles.*

What is it tell me?

GIRL ONE *giggles.*

Are you drunk?

GIRL ONE *jumps a little.*

Are you high?

GIRL ONE. I've got love eggs inside me.

GIRL TWO. What?

GIRL ONE. Love eggs? Vibrating eggs. They're a sex toy?

GIRL TWO. A what?

GIRL ONE. God you're such a square. A sex toy? You know? For pleasure? Two eggs, that you put up your vulva, so they nestle next to your clit and then you press this little button.

She brandishes a little remote control.

And they vibrate and massage… stuff and it feels…

She giggles.

GIRL TWO. Oh my god, stop it. That is so inappropriate.

GIRL ONE. No it isn't. It's good.

GIRL TWO. What happens if they, like crack, inside you?

GIRL ONE. They're made of rubber, you dork.

GIRL TWO. I am sorry, I don't need eggs, I am actually having sex tonight –

GIRL ONE. It's funny cos being a product of IVF, I would think the imagery of eggs would kill my excitement, you know?

GIRL TWO *groans.*

But I've had them in all morning and it has been… fun. You should get some, they are really portable and come in all sorts of colours. Mine are glow in the dark, look.

She shows a little remote.

GIRL TWO. Keep that cum-stained contraption away from me.

GIRL ONE. It's just the remote.

GIRL TWO. No seriously, leave me alone, weirdo.

GIRL ONE. Well, excuse me for wanting to add a little spark to the drudgery of dog-walking.

GIRL TWO. Aren't you meant to have, like, ten dogs on you now?

GIRL ONE. I like to let them roam free, really stretch their legs.

GIRL TWO. Don't you worry they might get run over?

GIRL ONE. Ah, who cares, this is my last week.

GIRL TWO. Why? Have you finally got an exhibition?

GIRL ONE *turns off the eggs.*

GIRL ONE. No. The team leader said my attitude was all wrong. That I've 'lost my dedication'.

GIRL TWO. To what?

GIRL ONE. To everything. Apparently.

GIRL TWO. Ah, that's not true. You love those dogs. Wherever they are.

GIRL ONE. I mean, I probably have been a bit… reckless lately.

Pause.

I lost Rachel from S Club 7's basset hound.

GIRL TWO. You walk Rachel from S Club 7's basset hound?

GIRL ONE. Until I lost it.

GIRL TWO. She has a basset hound? Weird.

GIRL ONE. Anyway, Waffles was fine. So.

GIRL TWO. Oh god, that could have been terrible.

GIRL ONE. See you always do that, take the other side. It's so annoying.

GIRL TWO. Oh right, thanks. Then why do you keep begging to hang out with me?

GIRL ONE *(suddenly warm)*. I want to chat, catch up, gossip, whatever. We never see each other any more.

GIRL TWO. We see each other all the time.

GIRL ONE. Not like we used to, not like the uni days.

GIRL TWO. We lived together at uni.

GIRL ONE. We only live round the corner from each other now.

GIRL TWO. I have a full-time job. It's different. Some of us don't have time to just lay about drinking, dressed as nineties' icons.

GIRL ONE. I resent that. I have a hectic schedule, it just isn't defined by some ruthless corporation.

GIRL TWO. I'm just saying, you haven't done a proper exhibition for, like… a while.

GIRL ONE. How can you say that? You've just seen my new work?

GIRL TWO *is blank*.

My performance? At Rose's?

GIRL TWO. Oh. That.

GIRL ONE. Yeah. I am a powerful performer, don't you think?

GIRL TWO. I didn't really get to see it, cos I had to help out at the bar, for most of the night.

GIRL ONE. Really? Why?

GIRL TWO. All her friends are meant to.

GIRL ONE. Well being her oldest friend, and the only remotely artistic one of the group, it's natural that I provide the entertainment.

GIRL TWO. Yeah. I am not sure how appropriate it was this year, but –

GIRL ONE. Um, it was about the absurdity of grief. How much more appropriate can you get?

GIRL TWO. It was… very long.

GIRL ONE. Can a eulogy to one's dead best friend ever be too long.

GIRL TWO. Yes. And how can you make a… rap piece? Confronting grief? You've never confronted it in real life.

GIRL ONE. Look, we all deal with that stuff differently.

GIRL TWO. Clearly. You deal with it on stage.

GIRL ONE. Potato, *patata*.

GIRL TWO. No one says *patata*.

Pause.

GIRL ONE. Remember when you dragged me and Rose to your, like, end-of-term seminar? Straight from that house party?

GIRL TWO. Ha, yes my 'Women's History' module. The lecturer was so scared of looking sexist, he didn't say anything.

GIRL ONE. Even though we'd taken so much mephedrone, we smelled like a garden centre.

GIRL TWO. Oh, for a mephedrone-laced lunch!

GIRL ONE. Amen.

Pause.

Well. How is your high-powered career going?

GIRL TWO. Don't pretend like you give a shit about my job.

GIRL ONE. I do. You work in… an office.

GIRL TWO. Nice try. I just got a promotion, actually.

GIRL ONE. There we go, great!

GIRL TWO. No, it's a disaster. I keep trying to leave, remember? Meet a husband, build a family? But every time I mention it, they just offer me more money.

GIRL ONE. Wait, what do you mean, 'leave'?

You are, like, the most hard-working person I know.

GIRL TWO. Well, that says more about your social life than my work ethic. But for a while now, I have begun to realise that the job I want to do, the one I was, in fact, born to do, is to have children.

GIRL ONE. Wow. That's… backward.

GIRL TWO. You've no idea what it is like. You've never had a nine-to-five in your life. And you've certainly never had a pervert boss like mine.

GIRL ONE. Sounds dreamy to me, I'll take a pervert any day.

GIRL TWO. He has these massive moist thumbs, which he's always massaging me with. He sort of prods them into my ears. It's, like, the most invasive thing ever.

GIRL ONE. Wow, ear rape. How do you report that shit?

GIRL TWO. It's awkward, you know? Cos his wife works with us too. And I'm like, 'Hello, this is not my fault.'

GIRL ONE. What's not your fault?

GIRL TWO. It puts me in a difficult position, being so young and attractive and female.

GIRL ONE. Tough.

GIRL TWO. It is, in the workplace. Cos the older career women, they look at me, this sexually ripe… peach and they assume, wrongly, that I am going to use my youth and beauty to get ahead.

GIRL ONE. Didn't you fuck the CEO once in a disabled loo at, like, a charity Easter-egg-hunt thing?

GIRL TWO. Jesus. If I was a man that would not still be an issue. It is so disrespectful.

GIRL ONE *laughs*.

I am unbelievably good at my job. I do not need to sleep with people to get ahead.

GIRL ONE. You just, conveniently, did.

Pause.

GIRL TWO. Maybe I am more of a guy's girl? I have always got on better with men. They like me. Women are just so… competitive. And older women are like… broken sculptures.

Pause.

GIRL ONE. Yeah. But I doubt that they are actually that jealous of you, though. Cos I mean, you're a bit neurotic and insecure.

GIRL TWO (*smiling, despite herself*). Sorry, are you talking to a mirror?

GIRL ONE (*enjoying the ritual*). And you're not even that young.

GIRL TWO. Look at my complexion. Flawless.

GIRL ONE. And it's not like you are in a relationship.

GIRL TWO. Well that is going to change tonight, so.

GIRL ONE. Oh? Are you going on a date?

GIRL TWO. Sort of, I am going to Lauren's party, why aren't you coming?

GIRL ONE. I hate Lauren.

GIRL TWO. Ah, I am so excited. I haven't been out in ages and I just know that I am going to meet someone. You know how you just know sometimes? You know?

GIRL ONE. No.

GIRL TWO. I have waxed my entire body. I didn't mean to. I was just doing my underarms and then, like, the pain, sort of numbed my nerves, and before I knew what had happened, I was a Barbie.

GIRL ONE. I'm growing out my pubic hair. Why should I relentlessly try and conform with some male fantasy of the shaved-female image?

GIRL TWO. Cos armpit hair is rank.

GIRL ONE. It actually feels fine. It looks cool too, soon I'll be able to braid it.

She lifts her arm up.

GIRL TWO. Alright, Cousin Itt. You're reminding me of my mum. I'm leaving.

GIRL ONE. What? No, don't leave me. Please?

GIRL TWO. I think you should be worrying about where your dogs are at.

GIRL ONE. Alright fine. But call me tomorrow? Let me know how your imaginary man likes his plastic bride.

GIRL TWO. Whatever, lonely egg girl. You need to get the real thing up there once in a while. Seriously.

GIRL ONE. I am an autonomous, independent, sexually self-satisfied being.

GIRL TWO. Autonomous?

She grabs the remote and presses it.

GIRL ONE shudders, alarmingly, squealing in forced pleasure.

GIRL ONE. Ah. Ah. Okay. Okay. Stop.

GIRL TWO chucks back the remote.

Bye.

GIRL TWO. Bye.

GIRL ONE (*hearing a bark and seeing something in the distance*). Mel B, heel!

Sound and light fill the stage.

Scene Four

A café. May. 2015.

GIRL TWO. I think I am a stalker.

GIRL ONE. What?

GIRL TWO. No, really I am an incredibly efficient stalker, like a hunt dog.

GIRL ONE. Please don't confess to a hideous crime now. I'm too fragile. I had a lot of cider and ketamine last night.

GIRL TWO. I didn't even know people still did ketamine.

GIRL ONE. Oh, at hunt balls they do! Fresh from the stables, as it were.

GIRL TWO. You're so weird and rural.

GIRL ONE. And poor. Will you buy me a coffee?

GIRL TWO. What? No, get your own coffee.

GIRL ONE. I can't afford that, soya, frappa crap. It's like four quid, such a rip-off.

GIRL TWO. But you can afford horse tranquilliser?

GIRL ONE. That stuff is like fifty pee a tonne, anyway, I didn't buy it.

GIRL TWO. Have you ever bought your own drugs?

GIRL ONE. Being an artist in this capitalist hellhole of a city is crippling. You have no idea what it is like.

GIRL TWO. Every day's a hustle, I am sure.

Pause.

Fine.

GIRL ONE *jumps up and kisses* GIRL TWO.

Ergh. KEEP AWAY! You stink.

Pause.

So, as I was saying.

GIRL ONE. You're a stalker, yeah, I have always known that.

GIRL TWO. I mean, I only just met him at Lauren's party.

GIRL ONE *pulls a face.*

And well, I don't know what came over me, I think it was the stress of the last few weeks, you know?

GIRL ONE *is blank.*

Anyway, for whatever reason, I got incredibly pissed at the party and ended up giving him...

(*Whispering.*) A blow job, so unlike me. It was really embarrassing –

GIRL ONE. Yeah it really is. Ha, where did you do the deed?

GIRL TWO. Behind that stupid bike-shed thing, who actually has a bike-shed in London?

GIRL ONE. I know, Lauren's so anal.

GIRL TWO. And now I can't stop staring and praying that my phone will suddenly ting, or vibrate, depending on my work situation, and that he will end my torment and finally let me know that he remembers the girl who clamped her lips around his...

(*Whispering.*) Semi-erect penis.

GIRL ONE. Ha.

GIRL TWO. It's not funny. Do you realise I have literally, no not literally, that implies untruth or exaggeration for effect, I have actually masturbated thrice every day this week.

GIRL ONE. Thrice?

GIRL TWO. Sometimes more, just to release my nervous energy. I can't deal with this. I am a busy woman, I can't be wasting my time… thus… I mean I pride myself on my rational, mature, together approach to life and yet: Boom! I am a teenager, barricaded in my bedroom.

She looks around the café and whispers again.

Now That's What I Call Music 41 masking the noise as I make myself cum and cum.

GIRL ONE. Why are you whispering? I mean it is a bit weird that you listen to *Now That's What I Call Music 41* but you don't need to be ashamed.

GIRL TWO. There are kids playing.

She gestures to the families all around.

And I just happened to be looking through my old CDs and *Now That's What I Call Music 41* actually has some really good artists, like Planet Perfecto?

GIRL ONE. Who the hell are Planet Perfecto?

GIRL TWO. You know?

(*Sings, quietly.*) 'It's not over, it's not over, not over…'

GIRL ONE. Oh yeah.

GIRL ONE *also sings, they both get much louder.* GIRL ONE *raucously so.*

'It's not over, not over yet…'

Ha, highly appropriate.

She sings again but this time in orgasmic manner.

'It's not… oovverrr, not oovverrr not o-o-o-ovverrr yeeeet.'

GIRL TWO. Stop it!

GIRL ONE. God I haven't been to a good nineties' night for ages. We used to go all the time at uni. Remember our Hallowe'en party in second year? The routine?

GIRL TWO. Oh my god! Yes! The *Romy and Michele High School Reunion* routine. Rose was Romy, the cool one, of course, I was Michele, the hot one, and you were the geek boy Sandy Frink. Ha.

GIRL ONE. You were meant to be Sandy Frink, but you kicked up such a fuss about being a man. How very gender normative of you.

GIRL TWO. You don't even know what that means!

Her phone beeps, she jumps up, very overexcited.

Oh it's just my creepy boss.

(*Whispering again.*) The other slightly weird thing is… when I am, you know?

She does an oddly graphic hand gesture.

GIRL ONE. Wanking?

GIRL TWO. Shhhhhh.

(*Whispering.*) Yes. When I am…

She does the graphic hand gesture again.

The odd thing is, that as I really get going, you know, right up there, I start imagining me, him and a succession of older, random weirdos from my past. Like the fat, balding, middle-aged man who once temped at the reception for our university swimming pool? –

GIRL ONE. Ahhh –

GIRL TWO. Keeps coming to my mind. As I am cumming.

GIRL ONE. Oh come now?

GIRL TWO. It's like the grosser the imaginary orgy, the better I cum? Do you get that?

GIRL ONE. Er, no!

GIRL TWO. Oh my god. What is happening to me? I am becoming obsessed and weird. I am becoming you.

GIRL ONE. Oh thanks. Excuse me, I'm not interested in guys who don't call me back.

Pause.

GIRL TWO. Bullshit.

GIRL ONE. Ha! Yeah, I know but god it felt good saying it. I wish I could play it cool like, like Monique. She's so blasé.

GIRL TWO. Yeah, but she's French.

GIRL ONE. True. Okay, well then like Scarlett Johansson. She's so cool.

GIRL TWO. She is cool but with those lips and tits, no one is ever not going to call her back.

GIRL ONE. Oh right, yeah. She has 'SA', as my grandmother would say.

GIRL TWO. What, a disease?

GIRL ONE. No, 'Sex Appeal'.

GIRL TWO. Oh, that. I think 'Sex Appeal' is really just a fertility thing.

GIRL ONE. Hardly.

GIRL TWO. A man looks at you and those motherly, child-bearing hips, and thinks, 'Take me now and let's fertilise those eggs.'

GIRL ONE. Lucky lady.

GIRL TWO. Yeah. He can't help it, he's genetically programmed to think like that. That's why Nigella's so successful, cos she's curvy AND she cooks.

GIRL ONE. Yeah, men cream themselves thinking about all the babies she could bake in that womb.

GIRL TWO. My womb is getting ready to have a baby.

GIRL ONE. God, stop saying this.

GIRL TWO. I am a year and a half older than you. You'll feel the same way too one day. It's biology.

GIRL ONE. Er, with my mum's fertility record? Not likely… IVF children are –

GIRL TWO. Boring, heard it all before. Just you wait.

GIRL ONE. No. Thanks. Women only have children to fill a void left by a society that fetishises youth. It's a massive vanity project designed to keep women feeling loved and needed when they've been passed over by everyone else.

GIRL TWO. That is just so… not true.

GIRL ONE. Hey, I get it. No one wants to be old and lonely.

GIRL TWO. By the time you realise how wrong you are, it will be too late.

Pause.

GIRL ONE. Cher.

GIRL TWO. Who?

GIRL ONE. In her nineties'-dance phase. You must remember the video for 'Believe'? Rose used to love it. She was like, an alien in a glass cage. So pretty cool. But, actually, she was really fiery. She'd, like, turn back time if someone didn't call her back. She looks cold though, sort of pinched, taut, you know?

GIRL TWO. Yeah, it's called plastic surgery.

GIRL ONE. Ah.

GIRL TWO (*looking at her phone*). Oh my god!

GIRL ONE. What?

GIRL TWO. He still hasn't messaged me, this is unbearable.

GIRL ONE. Just get in fucking touch.

GIRL TWO. I know. I know. It's just I have started to be a bit reticent about the whole, taking-charge thing, lately. Because, well, various ex-boyfriends have told me, after we broke up, that my overwhelming enthusiasm and passion at the beginning of our relationship sort of well, overwhelmed them and blinded them to the fact that we, in fact, had nothing in common.

GIRL ONE. Ouch.

GIRL TWO. Yeah and so it's sort of made me rethink my ideas about the breaking-down of gender roles, cos even though I am empowered to chase a guy, and time is of the essence and all, it usually leads me to be with insecure fuck-ups who suck me dry like a vampire.

GIRL ONE. Point taken.

GIRL TWO. Yeah, but I am also really impatient and impulsive so ahhhhhhh, I'll just message him now.

GIRL ONE. What? No. Wait!

GIRL TWO. Oops too late. Do you think that bicycle emoji was a bit much?

Sound and light fill the stage.

Scene Five

A supermarket. August. 2015.

GIRL ONE. You never reply to my texts. You never answer my calls. What, do you see it's me and just reject them?

GIRL TWO. Sorry, what are you doing here? Have you been following me?

GIRL ONE. No, I always shop here, at this time.

GIRL TWO. You always shop at this vegan supermarket at 8 p.m.? What for?

GIRL ONE (*looking about her*). Quorn. Mainly.

She grabs a packet of nearby Quorn.

And the few times I have managed to get through to you, you just go on about how busy you are.

GIRL TWO. I am. I don't see anyone, work is really demanding.

GIRL ONE. That's not true, you are always going out.

GIRL TWO (*texting*). What are you talking about, like where?

GIRL ONE. Can you stop looking at your phone?

GIRL TWO. Sorry. I am expecting a work call. Where?

GIRL ONE. Olivia's party.

GIRL TWO. She was leaving to go live in Moscow, of course I went.

GIRL TWO's phone vibrates and she instantly goes back to it.

GIRL ONE. Anna's dinner?

GIRL TWO. She lives next door to me, it was hardly 'a dinner'.

GIRL ONE. There were seven guests, that's a party.

GIRL TWO. Okay, are you stalking me?

GIRL ONE. No! I mean, yes. Look, I know that you have just fallen in love. With old 'Blow Job Bike-shed', who would've thought it?

And I am so happy for you. I just, I am a bit sad sometimes, from time to time, at the moment. And I – need – would like – to talk to you about it and instead… I feel a bit left out. AND I KNOW YOU ARE TEXTING HIM!

GIRL TWO. Sorry. Left out? From what, a threesome? Look, you're not left out. Well you are from that, we don't do that. I haven't ever. It's not that I'm a prude, it is just that I haven't needed to, not that you need. Mmm.

Pause.

Anyway the point is, I am sorry if I have been a little distant. It's only been a few months, we're in the honeymoon period. Look, don't worry, it will fall apart soon and I'll come crawling back to you all alone and depressed. I love you, I'm always here for you…

Looking at her phone and giggling.

How many emojis can he cram onto a screen? Look.

GIRL ONE is stony-faced.

Oh, come on, you know what it's like?

GIRL ONE. Apparently not, according to you.

GIRL TWO. Oh please. Is this about the Swiss wimp? He was not your boyfriend.

GIRL ONE. No. It's just, lately, I have been in a bit of a… rut. You know stopping dog-walking –

GIRL TWO. Well I think it was about time you left –

GIRL ONE. Exactly, it's the time, all the time I now have with my thoughts. My weird little thoughts. And things have got, well, weirder –

GIRL TWO. I doubt that's possible –

GIRL ONE. I am actually starting to look in at office windows and see all those idiotic little drones, sitting at their desks, and I'm thinking like, 'I wish I was a drone, at a desk, crunching someone else's numbers for a corporation who doesn't give a shit.'

I'm actually thinking that.

GIRL TWO. Thanks a lot for calling me a drone.

GIRL ONE. Don't get me wrong, I wish I could, like you, I wish I could be satisfied with the mundane minutiae of life.

GIRL TWO. What the fuck?

GIRL ONE. Yeah you know money, restaurants, girly nights out, nails, a two-point-four family: bourgeois shit.

GIRL TWO. You are such a dick.

GIRL ONE. Look this is not about you. I just feel so futile. And if I am not doing… What am I?

GIRL TWO. Well get a job then, Jesus, you've been educated enough.

GIRL ONE. I keep thinking about how I am a product of IVF?

GIRL TWO. Not this again –

GIRL ONE. I am definitely not meant to be here, my mum had to try and try and try and this was in the eighties, this was serious sci-fi shit then. Her eggs were extracted from her, examined, hormoned and finally, put into another woman's womb. If this was my grandmother's day, I just wouldn't have been born, I wouldn't be here.

GIRL TWO. Neither would most of us. Coughs killed people –

GIRL ONE. It has just embedded itself in me, this thought, and I can't flush it out. I am an experiment, a test-tube baby –

GIRL TWO. You are a test-tube baby, but that's fine –

GIRL ONE. An experiment that hasn't worked, a Frankenstein. Not a woman, not a desirable, fecund, normal woman but a barren vessel, who won't be able to have children, like my barren mother –

GIRL TWO. Stop it –

GIRL ONE. These thoughts, they're so negative –

GIRL TWO. Oh my god. Get a grip. The world has negative thoughts. Look at the news, for once. We all hate each other. Everyone lives in fear of everyone else. Of being blown up on their way to work. Or of being shot by a policeman for wearing a hoodie. Or of being beheaded by some bloke called John. It's… depressing but normal, sadly. Have you tried Xanax?

As GIRL ONE *speaks, the faint sound of string music can be heard.*

GIRL ONE. These thoughts; breeding in me. Lately, walking in a crowd, I'll close my eyes and lightly step off the pavement. I anticipate the impact, the cold, hard thwack that would knock me up and onto the road, landing with a crack. My skull cracking open, my brain splurging out, oozing out like an… omelette. But just as I can smell the wheels, feel the destruction, some archaic instinct aches into action and drags me back onto the street. And I am relieved, I am really, really relieved. Glad to be saved, to be alive. A happy hypocrite. But what happens, what happens when one day that instinct stops working?

The music stops.

GIRL TWO. Sorry, is this one of your monologues? I can't tell any more.

Sound and light fill the stage.

Scene Six

An art gallery in a garage. November. 2015.

GIRL TWO *claps*. GIRL ONE *has obviously just finished a performance*.

GIRL TWO. Wow. It was… even longer.

GIRL ONE. Thanks. Cool space, no?

GIRL TWO. Yeah, it's… a lovely garage.

GIRL ONE. One of the artists is squatting in it, it's her mum's.

GIRL TWO. Oh.

Pause.

Hey, happy belated birthday!

GIRL ONE. Feeling guilty for missing my party, are you?

GIRL TWO. What do you mean 'party'? What party?

GIRL ONE. My '*Female Singers of the Nineties*' party? I still can't believe how many people came dressed as Dannii Minogue, she used to be so much more –

GIRL TWO. I didn't hear anything about your party.

GIRL ONE. What? Yes you did. The hilarious e-invite?

GIRL TWO. I didn't get one.

GIRL ONE. Oh. God. Um. I probably assumed you were too busy working?

GIRL TWO. Yeah.

Pause.

Glad I could make it today, though. I didn't realise it would be so far out –

GIRL ONE. I always feel like I am going to be picked up in an art gallery. Some bearded… man, or woman, probably the artist, sees me from across the room and is profoundly and inexplicably moved.

GIRL TWO. Definitely inexplicably.

GIRL ONE (*looking around the art exhibition*). I think that most of my actions are motivated by the fact that I hope to be picked up by someone. That's like, my main motivation for doing most things. To be picked up.

(*Pointing to a sculpture*.) Isn't this piece opaque?

GIRL TWO *struggles to comprehend*.

GIRL TWO. Any luck?

GIRL ONE. Sort of. I had near-sex with someone last night.

GIRL TWO. 'Near'? Why does that not surprise me?

GIRL ONE. In so far as we ended up completely naked on his mum's sofa. Well I was completely naked, he kept his polo neck on, but the important half was bare as a baby.

GIRL TWO. Ewww.

GIRL ONE. It was nice. We fingered each other. I love being fingered, don't you? Beats everything else if you ask me.

GIRL TWO. I didn't.

GIRL ONE. Luckily so, cos then he attempted to lick me out, but my pubic hair has all kind of matted now so, no. And by the time we graduated to sex, he was pretty out of it and it all sort of… flopped. Yeah. Probably for the best, good to take things slow.

GIRL TWO. Who did you 'drug' into doing this?

GIRL ONE. Well, actually this might sound quite weird, so don't freak out but it was with – (*Whispering*.)

GIRL TWO. Whaaaaaaat? What the fuck? What? No.

GIRL ONE. I knew you'd be weird about this. You always drag –

GIRL TWO. He was Rose's first boyfriend.

GIRL ONE. Yeah, when they were like fourteen.

GIRL TWO. Seventeen. Don't you find that weird? Like getting with your sister's boyfriend?

GIRL ONE. That would never happen, she only dates property developers.

GIRL TWO. And what about Lucy?

GIRL ONE. What about her?

GIRL TWO. She's his girlfriend of four years.

GIRL ONE. Yeah, but he was my friend, well Rose's friend, first.

GIRL TWO. What are you, like ten?

GIRL ONE. I introduced them.

GIRL TWO. But she's your friend. You like her.

GIRL ONE. I know, I know, it's just, you know, there has
always been so much love between us. Everyone says it,
even Rose would joke about it.

GIRL TWO. So what, are you going to be together? This is so
weird.

GIRL ONE. Fuck off. I have been alone for a really long time.
And the relationships I have had have been…
unconventional.

GIRL TWO. So are you two going to be boyfriend and
girlfriend?

GIRL ONE. I don't know. We were quite drunk and when I
woke up he had already left for work.

GIRL TWO. I see.

GIRL ONE. I haven't been this happy in so, so long. I don't feel
so bleak or like I want to hurt a stranger –

GIRL TWO. Woo –

GIRL ONE. It's like, the world has… rose-tinted specs on
again.

GIRL TWO. I just don't –

GIRL ONE. I think I might be in love. I might finally be in love.

GIRL TWO. I think he is cheating on me. We never have sex and
he keeps having work lunches with a girl who has just started
at his office. The other day, I bumped into them on the street –

GIRL ONE. God you really are a good stalker! –

GIRL TWO. And the look on his face was just, pure scared shame. After six months. Only six months.

Pause.

She's not even pretty. She is short, squat, stubby even.

When I go to a party, people text me after to say how much they enjoyed speaking to me, how engaging I was. They like me, I am a hit. Not too in-your-face, but punchy, flirtatious but in a non-threatening way. Magnetic. Eloquent and still a tiny bit street, both confusing the poshos and intriguing the hipsters. Intelligent but nothing heavy. Sparky. And no one can believe I am nearly thirty. No one. I know because I play this little game where I get people to guess my age, people love it, and without exception they all presume I am in my early to mid-twenties. Not a line on my face, hair, bouncy and luscious, eyes like Nutella, body as tight as a… whistle.

She whistles.

And. Oh fuck it. I was just about to do it. Breeze through it. Smash through the brick wall that is thirty. Secure, smug and snug as a bug in a rug or whatever and then, then? That short, fat, fucking stub of a Thumbelina has to come into my life and, I don't know? Wow him with her innate ability to give him a blow job standing up?

Breaking down, crying.

Oh fuck it, fuck it, fuck it.

Sound and light fill the stage.

Scene Seven

Sitting room. December. 2015.

Mica Levi's 'Love' plays through out this scene.

GIRL ONE *is on the phone to* GIRL TWO, *who is rushing around, preparing a dinner.*

GIRL ONE. Have you seen *Under the Skin*?

GIRL TWO. Are you calling for anything in particular this time? Cos I've got friends coming over for a Christmas dinner in an hour.

GIRL ONE. Oh.

Pause.

GIRL TWO. It's a work-ish thing. You'd –

GIRL ONE. So have you seen it? Cos I think you would really connect to it too. You know, cos it's about being alone –

GIRL TWO. Alone, what are you talking about? –

GIRL ONE. Scarlett Johansson, plays an alien who just drives around some rank town like Swansea, or Slough? Picking up men in a van, taking them back to her lair, where she does a striptease and then kills them in a vat of space oil and the whole time she is wearing, like, Primark.

GIRL TWO. Primark, really?

GIRL ONE. Yeah, she looks all normal and chubby with, like, a flabby belly, a brown wig and kitten-heel boots.

GIRL TWO. Errr!

GIRL ONE. And it just made so much sense to me, cos that's it. That's what I have been trying to explain to you. I feel like such an alien. A hatched thing. This creature who has the shell of a woman but inside is just this weird little alien, just taking it all in, totally confused by everything. Unable to really understand what the fuck anyone means.

GIRL TWO. Isn't that what Scientologists believe, that we are all aliens?

GIRL ONE. I am serious, like, I don't understand humankind, women, friends, men, lovers. I literally have no idea. And I

never have. Just like Scarlett Johansson, I can look, seem,
right but in fact know nothing and understand no one and –

GIRL TWO. So what, you'd be Scarlett Johansson in this
scenario?

GIRL ONE. He didn't even mention it, he never phoned. It's
been weeks! I finally saw him at a drinks party I was
waitressing at. I had an apron on!

GIRL TWO. Ouch.

GIRL ONE. I threw down my tray and walked straight up to
him and you know what he said? He said it was too weird,
because of Rose. 'Too weird'? They went out ten years ago!
Then he scuttled back to Lucy, clamped his arm around her
waist. The coward. Then she, she came up, kissed me, on the
cheek… I –

GIRL TWO. Look, it was always going to be a sensitive –

GIRL ONE. I wish I'd actually fucked him, you know? Then I
would've been able to be legitimately mad, to have really
made a scene. But a bit of mutual masturbation? It just
sounds lame if I bring it up.

Pause.

Shall we go? Like right now, find some strangers and have
actual sex? It would cheer us both up, no? Being lonely is
so shit!

GIRL TWO. What are you talking about, I am not lonely. I am
in a committed, mature relationship?

GIRL ONE. But what about the Thumbelina?

GIRL TWO (*laughing, maniacally*). Oh, her. No. No. I was just
feeling, so silly, insecure about my relationship. Mad, even.
No. The moment we sat down and talked about it, I realised I
was being totally irrational and, more than that, I was being
unfair, to us. Because rather than ask him, I just harboured
these negative accusations, which, once he had the
opportunity to defend himself, seemed ludicrous. Innocent
until proven guilty. The girl is married and is French, which
is why they are always meeting up. Because she is teaching
him French, which his boss says he needs for the Paris

office, he wanted it to be a surprise, we are moving to Paris. We have never been so great, we're so much more respectful, mature –

GIRL ONE. No sex, sex, sex, sex, sex sex, sex. I am going mad. I've started walking around the streets. Cruising the streets, like Scarlett. Fat, little Scarlett. No dogs, just me, in a Uniqlo puffer, walking, eyeing men. I've definitely freaked a couple out. I have quite intense eyes. But when I do make eye contact, what then? I am not a prostitute, or Scarlett, I am just a well-spoken, strawberry-blonde from Sussex. I can't actually approach them. I'd get mugged. Then I am like, 'Maybe I'll call a prostitute', but that's even worse. Desperate. Only pudgy businessmen and women with receding hairlines need to pay for it? Then I think, 'Just phone a friend.' A good old booty call. But what if, what if they say:

'No'?

'Oh, I don't think of you that way.'

'Who do you think you are, you fat, fugly, freak. As if.'

GIRL TWO. Look, if it's sex you want, though I think counselling is what you really need, why don't you just go on a night out with some friends and like, flirt, people are always having drunken sex which they regret on nights out… it's easy.

GIRL ONE. No. I feel too distant from my generation to go out.

GIRL TWO. Listen to yourself!

GIRL ONE. They say that most crimes are performed by sexually frustrated men on a largely sugar-based diet.

Pause.

I eat a lot of Maoams.

GIRL TWO. Okay, I am not quite clear where this is heading?

GIRL ONE. Do you, do you ever… when you see a pregnant woman, on a train or waiting next to you at a bus stop, so she's side on to you, her rotund stomach, protruding past you… her belly button, poking out prominently… her smooth, plastic skin, stretched like canvas, or clay, around her new life form. Firm yet so, so delicate. Fragile. When you see her, do you sometimes get an urge, an uncontrollable urge to stab her, right there, in the belly? To puncture that round, taut ball? With an iron rod or better yet, a bare, clenched, fist? The feeling of destruction, the warm, sweet, sticky destruction as both lives bleed out of her? Pump out of her? Wail out of her?

GIRL TWO. Oh my god, no. Stop talking now. I'm pregnant.

GIRL ONE. What? What do you mean?

GIRL TWO. I mean I am pregnant. So stop speaking.

GIRL ONE. What? Since when?

GIRL TWO. Since I found out last week. You're not meant to tell people –

GIRL ONE. I obviously didn't mean I would actually hurt anyone. You. I.

Pause.

Yay. Congratulations. I guess.

GIRL TWO. 'I guess'? Is that the best you can do?

GIRL ONE. You should call it Scarlett if it is a girl.

Sound and light fill the stage.

Scene Eight

A night club. New Year's Eve. 2015.

'Not Over Yet' by Planet Perfecto plays.

GIRL ONE *dances enthusiastically.* GIRL TWO *stands still, awkward.*

They are both dressed in nineties' clothing.

GIRL ONE. I can't believe your orgasm song is playing, how great is this?

She does the same orgasmic singing as before.

GIRL TWO. Stop it. When I said 'friends', I didn't mean me. I am pregnant. I shouldn't be at a club.

GIRL ONE. Oh come on, you're like a week pregnant. A couple of drinks and some MDMA are not going to hurt.

GIRL TWO. Where the hell are we? I thought Peckham was far, but this place? My Uber driver hadn't even heard of it.

GIRL ONE. Hey, I spent ages looking for a cool night for us to go to, stop being so negative.

GIRL TWO. I've never seen so many men in black mesh. They look like they've all just stepped out of art school.

GIRL ONE. Yeah, well, they sort of have.

GIRL TWO. What?

GIRL ONE. This night is run by Goldsmiths.

GIRL TWO. You brought me to a student night?

GIRL ONE. Oh come on, they are not all that young. Anyway it's not term-time so technically it's not –

GIRL TWO. Oh my god. These children weren't even born in the nineties.

GIRL ONE. No, they were. Circa 1995, probably.

GIRL TWO. Oh my god, these children were BORN in the nineties. YOU ARE SO YOUNG!

GIRL ONE. Stop it. I am meeting a Tinder date here. Please don't go around shouting at people. Come on, let's get a drink.

GIRL TWO. No, no I am not going to drink.

GIRL ONE. Oh, please. I can't drink alone.

GIRL TWO. Okay, so I should harm my unborn child so you don't have to drink alone?

GIRL ONE. Yes.

She turns to the barman. She returns with two shots.

Hey, the barman just gave us two tequila shots for free cos

'Your mate is hot.'

GIRL TWO. You're kidding?

GIRL ONE. This is so typical. I am meant to be the one on the pull.

GIRL TWO. I'm not on the pull. Did he say hot?

GIRL ONE. Yes and he's like the only guy here over nineteen. So unfair.

GIRL TWO. Don't be negative.

GIRL TWO does a cheers to the barman and takes a sip.

GIRL ONE finishes both shots.

GIRL ONE. Another? Can you give a little wink to the barman, we might get them for free again.

GIRL TWO. No way.

She winks at him.

GIRL ONE. Ha, it worked, you are on fire.

They get two more shots. GIRL TWO still only sips hers.

GIRL TWO. Ah, do you think anyone will think I am hot again after I give birth?

GIRL ONE. What, after your vagina is ripped in two and your stomach sags to your knees? I doubt it.

GIRL TWO. My vagina, my beautiful vagina. My colleague Naomi said hers was never the same.

GIRL TWO sips her shot again, a little more deeply.

Pause.

You know, it's not like I am not scared. I have a life force growing inside me, living off me, stealing my life, my youth.

GIRL ONE. Like a nit?

GIRL TWO. Exactly. You know that breast milk is just blood without the red blood cells. I'm giving birth to a vampire.

She sucks.

GIRL ONE. An alien.

GIRL TWO. *Rosemary's Baby.* And the birth, the pain. I'll never be the same! Oh god.

She looks down.

Pause.

Two more shots for my beautiful minge!

They do two more shots.

And, like, I do love my job. Despite the pervs and battle axes. I am good at it.

GIRL ONE. Well mothers can still work? I mean mine didn't… But yours did.

GIRL TWO. No. I have given in my notice. Finally. We feel it would be better for the baby, if one of us is home all the time.

GIRL ONE. What the fuck, no? You love that job. I love that job.

GIRL TWO. I don't want to be always stressed and resentful.

GIRL ONE. Now you'll just be bored and resentful and poor. Which is bad for all of us.

GIRL TWO. And what if I don't have it now and then later I have problems and can't have one?

GIRL ONE. Well, being a product of IVF myself –

GIRL TWO. Better not fuck with nature. That's what I say.

GIRL ONE. Don't talk like an American person.

GIRL TWO. Well, nature is strong and I am just hoping, trusting that when I am actually holding it, him, her, whatever, in my hands, these doubts will evaporate and my natural role will take over.

GIRL ONE. Like magic?

GIRL TWO. Plus his mum lives really near and does nothing so she can help loads.

GIRL ONE (*concerned*). You can still… not have it. No one will judge you. It's your decision. He probably doesn't even want it either.

GIRL TWO. What the fuck? Of course he does.

GIRL ONE. I'm just saying, most men don't want one till later, because they can. Where as you, tick-tock, tick-tock, tick-tock.

'Believe' by Cher plays.

GIRL ONE *looks at* GIRL TWO *excitedly.*

Ah, the ultimate alien!

GIRL TWO. You know you are a horrible little bitch and that is why no one likes you and you will die childless and alone?

GIRL ONE. Yup. I know.

(*Brightly.*) Hey, let's do the routine?

GIRL TWO. What? No way.

GIRL ONE. Oh come on? It's high time we showed these kids how it's done.

GIRL TWO. You do realise that we are now older than the characters were in the film?

GIRL ONE. Speak for yourself, Grandma, I'm still twenty-eight.

GIRL TWO. We can't. Not without Rose.

GIRL ONE. Of course we can. I'll do Sandy and Romy's parts. It'll be great.

GIRL TWO. No that's really weird. And impossible.

GIRL ONE. No it isn't. Look, please? Rose would have loved it. I'd love it.

GIRL TWO. Ah. Okay.

GIRL ONE. Great.

Pause.

(*In an American accent.*) 'Will you dance with me, Michele?'

GIRL TWO. I am not doing the intro.

GIRL ONE. Please?

(*In an American accent.*) 'Will you dance with me, Michele?'

GIRL TWO (*reluctantly, also in an American accent*). 'Only if Romy can dance with us.'

GIRL ONE. 'Sure.'

They begin a very loose imitation of the dance routine from Romy and Michele's High School Reunion.

It is definitely a dance for three and GIRL ONE *has to jump from position to position to cover Rose's moves.*

As the dance comes back to her, GIRL TWO *begins to get really into it, reliving her glory days as the hot, fun girl at university.*

At a certain point, however, GIRL ONE, *hit by the pathos of the moment, has to stop. She is literally dancing in her dead friend's footprints and the pathetic tragedy of the whole situation, her whole situation, is overwhelming.*

Ashamed of this moment of weakness, she quickly approaches a nearby man and starts to grind him, aggressively.

GIRL TWO *is left doing the routine alone, until she notices* GIRL ONE *has abandoned her. She stops, hurt, and starts to smile at the barman, coyly at first, then more forwardly. She responds to something he mouths to her. She is about to walk towards him when* GIRL ONE *notices and quickly returns to her, tapping her on the shoulder.*

GIRL TWO. What are you doing? I thought you were going to get with that guy?

GIRL ONE. He started dry-humping me.

GIRL TWO. You know what your problem is? You are way too contrary. Life is about compromise. Downsizing. Go to the toilets and fuck him.

GIRL ONE. I thought he was going to cum on my shin. What can I say? The romance died.

GIRL ONE *checks her phone.*

Oh my god. He's not coming.

GIRL TWO. What? Who?

GIRL ONE. My Tinder date.

(*Reading.*) 'Soz girl, Nunhead's not even in London. See ya in 2016.' Winky face.

GIRL TWO. Whoa.

GIRL ONE. No, I can't take this. This was my big night out and now it's ruined.

GIRL TWO. Hey, he's not worth it. Let's have another shot? The barman's promised me, like, five.

GIRL ONE (*coolly*). That didn't take long, did it?

GIRL TWO. What didn't?

GIRL ONE. Got them all lining up, haven't you?

GIRL TWO. What is that supposed to mean?

GIRL ONE. Nothing. It's just typical of you to be frantically pursuing all the attention you can desperately grasp.

GIRL TWO. Excuse me?

GIRL ONE. Like, you would shrivel up and die without the male gaze.

GIRL TWO. Why are you saying this?

GIRL ONE. Like the Wicked Witch in the *Wizard of Oz*:

'Ah, men aren't looking at me, help, Dorothy, I'm melting. I'm melting.'

GIRL TWO. You are so immature.

GIRL ONE. Oh god, forget it. I am going to take some MDMA in the toilets. I am too depressed to educate you, yet again.

GIRL TWO. How dare you. I came all the way to this kindergarten, for you.

GIRL ONE. Oh come on, you jumped at the offer. Probably hoping you might kill that baby with booze.

GIRL TWO. Oh my god.

GIRL ONE. Anything to stop you having to admit you don't really want it!

Pause.

GIRL TWO *is momentarily unable to speak.*

GIRL TWO. What is wrong with me? Why do I put up with this? We're not even friends.

GIRL ONE. Don't be ridiculous.

GIRL TWO. No. We were Rose's friends. And she's gone, a long time ago. So why am I still here? I don't even like you.

GIRL ONE. I have no idea, possibly cos you've bored the shit out of all your other friends, I mean, even Rose would bitch about you.

GIRL TWO. Fuck you.

GIRL ONE. Dunt!

GIRL TWO. When are you going to grow up and take responsibility for yourself and your pathetic little life? To wake up and realise that moaning, day in day out, is so, so, so boring. That singing badly over a nineties' rap song is not performance art… or even remotely enjoyable. And I don't care if it is meant to deliberately frustrate the viewer! That while you have been moping about, waiting for inspiration to thwack you on your talentless, privileged head, the world has moved on, life has moved on. And you have no right to judge those who have tried to move on with it. Or to leech off them for free food and twenty-four-hour mental-health care. That everyone loses people they love, has their heart broken. It's how they deal with it that counts. That you could have asked me, just once in all these fucking years, how I felt, sometimes. Cos I didn't feel great, a lot of the time. That having a child is a responsible, beautiful thing. IT'S NOT A VANITY PROJECT DESIGNED TO FILL A VOID LEFT BY SOCIETY. IT'S WHAT I WANT. IT'S WHAT I NEED. IT'S WHAT YOU WILL NEVER HAVE!

The music stops as the clock strikes 12 a.m. and the whole club starts to shout the countdown in unison. Dazed, GIRL ONE *and* GIRL TWO *join in, reluctantly.*

GIRL ONE *and* TWO. Ten, nine, eight, seven, six, five, four, three, two, one. Happy New Year! Happy 2016!

GIRL ONE *and* TWO *look at each other but do not embrace.*

GIRL TWO *walks out.*

GIRL ONE *is left. She looks around her.*

All at once the music and lighting in the club change. Mica Levi's 'Death' plays accompanied by a projection of Scarlett Johansson in Under the Skin, *stripping and killing her prey to the same music.*

The lights dim and a spotlight rests on GIRL ONE. *She turns to the audience and looks at them, picking out the men and eyeing them curiously, as though seeing a man for the first time.*

Her gaze lands on one in particular. She smiles at him. Then she slowly and methodically starts to undress for him. An absolutely straight striptease. Coat, shoes, jeans, shirt. She stands opposite him in her bra, beckoning him.

As GIRL TWO *re-enters, the lights and music change back to the clubbing sounds of before.*

GIRL TWO (*returning with her coat*). What the fuck are you doing?

GIRL ONE *ignores her, or doesn't hear her, and is looking ahead, dazed.*

Hello?

GIRL ONE *still does not respond.*

You know what? I am done.

GIRL TWO *exits.*

GIRL ONE *is left. In her underwear. Staring out at no one.*

Blackout. Silence.

Scene Nine

Hospital. March. 2016.

GIRL ONE *is lying on a bed.*

GIRL TWO *holds an Easter egg.*

GIRL TWO. I brought you an Easter egg?

GIRL ONE. Why?

GIRL TWO. I thought you might be hungry.

GIRL ONE. They feed me in here.

GIRL TWO. Because it's a tradition.

GIRL ONE. Well I am actually totally against the whole Easter-egg-tradition thing. So…

GIRL TWO. Oh god, fine. Cos work sent me, like, fifty.

GIRL ONE. I just think it is really warped that people celebrate the resurrection of Christ by gorging on chocolate replicas of potential life forms.

GIRL TWO. But it's chocolate. It's delicious.

GIRL ONE. It's carnivorous that's what it is. Especially when vegetarians do it. They should know better.

GIRL TWO. Right.

> *Pause.*

> So. It's been… a while.

> *Pause.*

> (*Brandishing the Easter egg.*) I am going back to my job. Hence…

> *Pause.*

GIRL ONE. I thought you hated it there?

GIRL TWO. Well, I've had –

GIRL ONE. I thought you didn't want to be a stressy bitch like your mum –

GIRL TWO. Well, I –

GIRL ONE. I thought you wanted to be a lobotomised Nigella, making cakes out of breast milk, or whatever you lot do.

GIRL TWO (*whispering*). Oh no.

Pause.

GIRL ONE. What?

GIRL TWO (*weakly*). I thought you would've heard.

GIRL ONE. Heard what?

Pause.

GIRL TWO. Well, you were right about one thing, at least.

He didn't want it, said I should 'get rid of it', 'better for us all'. That it was 'irrational' of me to want to have one after 'only being together a year or so'. That I'm 'too impulsive', 'impatient'.

'Passionate'. What the fuck? 'A year or so'? How long did he want me to wait?

GIRL ONE. What are you talking about?

GIRL TWO. Oh yeah and French lessons my fuck. The lying dickhead. Cheating little dickhead. I. He just came out with it:

'I don't love you. I never did. We're moving to France.'

'We're.'

Like they're an item. A double act. How dare they. He and She.

GIRL ONE. Oh my god. What are you going to do?

GIRL TWO. Rip his head off, that's what. Voodoo-doll him. Systematically contact his every acquaintance by email, listing his inadequacies.

GIRL ONE. What about your baby?

GIRL TWO. Don't call it that. It's not that yet, it's an embryo.

GIRL ONE. Um. What about your embryo, are you going to…?

GIRL TWO. To get rid of it? And give him what he wants? No. I'll have it. As a constant reminder, a ball and chain.

GIRL ONE. I really do not think that is a very positive way to think about bringing a child into the world. Really.

GIRL TWO. What am I supposed to do? Admit the mistake, blank it out? Let it all go?

GIRL ONE. You can't have a child to prove a point. It won't be happy, for you or it.

GIRL TWO. And what do you know about happiness?

GIRL ONE. Nice.

Pause.

GIRL TWO. Sorry… That wasn't very… Considering. Um. How are you?

GIRL ONE. Fine.

GIRL TWO *looks at her.*

I'm fine! Please don't say you spoke to my mum too? I accidentally drove off the road. That's all that happened, it was dark, I was –

GIRL TWO. You haven't even got a licence –

GIRL ONE. Reckless.

GIRL TWO. Fucking psychotic is what I call it.

GIRL ONE. Always so tactful.

GIRL TWO. Is your back okay? You're not going to have to be in a wheelchair?

GIRL ONE. God forbid! Look, it's just a bit bruised. It really was more of a bump than a crash.

GIRL TWO. You drove into the side of a school. / You could have hit a child. Imagine.

GIRL ONE. At 3 a.m. in Sussex. The place was deserted.

GIRL TWO. How could you do this to me?

GIRL ONE. Why do you give a shit? I thought we weren't friends any more?

GIRL TWO. Don't you dare. If I find out you did this to spite
me in some way –

GIRL ONE. Jesus. Your self-absorption knows no bounds –

GIRL TWO. I had to get a two-hour train out here. Were you
thinking of anyone but yourself? You selfish. Do you know
what it would mean if you had…

She cries.

Sorry you should be the one crying.

GIRL ONE. Why?

GIRL TWO. Oh god, you freak, because you are –

GIRL ONE. Look. I am fine.

GIRL TWO. No you are not. No it is not. No it hasn't been. No
it hasn't been.

Her cries escalate.

GIRL ONE *tentatively takes her hand.*

Pause.

GIRL TWO *gets into bed with* GIRL ONE *and curls up next
to her.*

Pause.

I am going to get rid of it next week. I have already booked
it. Signed its death warrant. I think.

Pause.

Will you come with me?

GIRL ONE. Yeah, course. If my mum ever allows me out of
here, that is.

GIRL TWO. I've thought about it a lot. I thought about you a
lot. You know how you're a product of IVF?

GIRL ONE. Allelujah, indeed.

GIRL TWO. Well, you turned out… psychotic… But okay too.
So I can always just fuck with nature.

GIRL ONE. Exactly. And you know, I'm always here for the harvesting.

They smile.

Pause.

GIRL TWO. Are we both doomed?

GIRL ONE. Potato, *patata*!

GIRL TWO. Tomato, *tamata*!

GIRL ONE (*blankly*). Let's call the whole thing off.

The End.

MR INCREDIBLE

Camilla Whitehill

Camilla Whitehill originally trained as an actor at the Birmingham School of Acting, graduating in 2012. She has had short plays produced at Soho Theatre, Park Theatre, Camden People's Theatre, the Old Red Lion, and the Hen & Chickens Theatre. Her short play *Icebergs* won the international short play competition Pint Sized Plays in 2013, and her radio play *Pier* was produced by the Heritage Arts Company. She was part of the Royal Court Young Writers' Programme in spring 2014, and is represented by Kitson Press Associates. Her first full-length play, *Where Do Little Birds Go?*, won the People's Choice Award at last year's VAULT Festival, completed a UK tour, and ran at the Underbelly at the Edinburgh Festival Fringe, where it gained critical acclaim and an almost completely sold-out run.

'Men are afraid that women will laugh at them.
Women are afraid that men will kill them.'

Margaret Atwood

'If the complainant (I do not refer to her as the victim)
was under the influence of alcohol or drugs, or both, when
she was 'raped', this provides the accused with a complete
defence. End of story and a victory for fairness, moderation
and common sense!'

*Top UK barrister David Osborne, in a blog post entitled
'She Was Gagging For It', February 2015*

Acknowledgements

I would like to thank Marina at Underbelly, Polaroid Theatre, Fine Mess Theatre, Jean Kitson at Kitson Press Associates, and the wonderful Mat, Tim and Andy from VAULT Festival for their help and support.

C.W.

Mr Incredible was first performed at VAULT Festival, London, on 10 February 2016, with the following cast:

ADAM   Alistair Donegan

Director	Sarah Meadows
Producer	Rosalyn Newbery
Designers	Justin Nardella and Catherine Morgan
Lighting Designer	Jamie Platt
Composer and Sound Designer	Benedict Taylor
Stage Manager	Laura Merryweather

Character

ADAM FREEMAN, *thirty-one*

Scene One

Nobody on stage. A chair with a jacket thrown over it. 'The Power of Goodbye' by Madonna plays over and over again on a thirty-second loop.

ADAM FREEMAN, *thirty-one, comes on, adjusting his belt. He notices the music and rushes over to grab his phone out of his jacket pocket. He presses a button. The music stops.*

Awkward pause.

Haha, sorry about that, that er
Haha
Did that, um
Was that playing for long?

He checks the screen.

Oh, eight missed calls. That's good. Just eight. Just eight looped choruses of 'The Power of Goodbye'
Which, is clearly
My ringtone
Bet you didn't know people still had songs as their ringtones, but, yep. Still very popular amongst thirteen-year-old girls and… me.

It reminds me of Holly
…I thought that would be a good excuse but actually it's just made it even sadder hasn't it
Got to keep it on silent. Last week it started playing in the dairy aisle at Tesco. I just acted like it wasn't me and pretended to be very interested in the soft cheeses.

Nice loos
By the way
Very nice. Cowshed. You can tell a lot about a company from the quality of their hand soap.
Sometimes it *looks* like fancy soap then you inspect it and you realise it's like, Morrison's own brand and you think, what are these people trying to hide

Anyway, sorry about that, I just suddenly realised that if I didn't go for a wee immediately something bad was going to happen. Crept up on me.

You were saying, er, what you were saying, sounds good. Very… good. Encouraging, even. I'm, er, I'm not that um

It's funny being here

Not funny, ha-ha, it's funny, unexpected. I'm not totally sure what to say. I'm usually great at talking, I talk a lot, Holly used to say I could talk my way out of an al-Qaeda beheading, nice image

Holly was the one who got me deeply into Madonna's back catalogue, specifically the *Ray of Light* album, which before you judge, is really

She told me one night that it was her favourite album *of all time*, and I really took the piss, so she made me get stoned with her and listen to it on repeat, and it turned out she was right, it is incredible and I was wrong. 'Frozen', mate. 'Frozen' is so good. *You're frozen… when your heart's not open* yeah I'm going to stop singing Madonna at you now, definitely. Yep.

She liked weird things, unpopular things, like she had this really hideous jumper with the Heinz Baked Beans logo on it. Which she would wear in public, like a weird hipster billboard with boobs. She wore it all the time even though she knew I hated it. She's quite, she's funny with stuff, she'd get attached to things, she once made me buy her a wonky lamp from a boot sale because it 'looked sad'. I've still got the bloody thing, can't seem to chuck it out.

I'm not talking about anything proper, am I

Sorry I'm just going to check my

He looks at his phone.

God, all those missed calls were from Neil. My flatmate. He moved in after

He's a bit of a cretin. Not really… my usual type, friendship-wise. But it was getting sort of quiet and depressing and he was one of the only people who

I'm very aware that I'm thirty-one and I have a flatmate, by the way. It's not that I necessarily need one. Although there is a

mortgage that needs paying, and I'm not, you know, not
working at the moment, er

Anyway everyone in *Friends* had a flatmate and they were
ancient.
Oh god, were they ancient? Or were they my age?
Shit. How old was Frasier?
No he actually was ancient. I need to calm down.

He looks at his phone again.

He's left a voicemail. Why? Who leaves voicemails any more?
Delete…

He puts his phone away. Pause.

You know how on weekends London suddenly becomes packed
full of smug couples? You know. Nicely dressed people holding
Whole Foods bags, snogging on park benches. Usually with a
dog. We were one of those couples. Me and Holly. Adam and
Holly. It even *sounds* right.

I'm just… not *meant* to be single.

Look – being honest, and not doing that faux-humble thing the
British love so much: I'm good looking, and I smell nice, and I
have a good job, a great, an interesting job. And I'm funny, ish,
or as funny as you need to be when you're already a nice-
smelling good-looking bloke, which as it turns out is not very.
People will laugh anyway.
I'm not trying to be a
I'm just being honest. Which is… what you wanted?
Yeah.

I live in Stoke Newington. Gorgeous garden flat. Preferred
living there with Holly, nothing spoils a gorgeous flat like
seeing Neil in his boxers every morning, but

I bought the flat about a year after I met Holly. My uncle died –
the only way anyone under forty buys property in London is if a
rich relative dies – my uncle died and I got money and I bought
the flat. And Holly wasn't interested, at first, in being involved.
She didn't like the idea of depending on anyone. Because she
wouldn't have been able to give very much to the mortgage, she
was an intern, and she was twenty-three and liked living with
her mates. Seemed very set on not moving in but then I showed

her round the place, you know… actual garden in London, fireplace in the bedroom, a *skylight* – everyone loves a skylight – and she changed her mind.
Anyone can be swayed by a nice skylight. Even Holly. Who never appears to care about anything… material, aesthetic.

She's very clever. She's
It could get quite
Girls like Holly are – I mean, it's exciting, it's interesting, always interesting, but they're never off, you know? Never quiet. You come home and you're knackered and they're never up for watching *Take Me Out*, which you know is shit but is still your favourite thing on telly. Holly would always be buzzing about something – the plight of the Syrian refugees or middle America's attitude to vaccinations – she's so clever, I wouldn't change that about her – but she didn't have that thing most of us have, where we pretend we're clever at work or when we're with other 'clever' people, but then when we get home we stop pretending and we start voting for *Celebrity Big Brother* on the iPhone app. She doesn't have that, her intelligence isn't a cover-up for anything, and the curse of that is she cares about *everything*, she is constantly outraged, she's like a human version of left-wing Twitter, always quoting articles and signing petitions and radiating indignation.

But she wrote for one of those magazines, those crap magazines that always have pictures of female celebrities in bikinis from bad angles on the front, the kind of magazine that Holly hated, hates, the kind of magazine she once ranted about for hours, but then she started writing for one
Because we say we won't compromise but then we have to pay deposits and bills and student loans and then

I mean she's also fun

I'm making her sound crap, she's not crap, she's fucking fun.
On my thirtieth birthday last year – god last year, is it that

Anyway we'd, well, we'd been having a rough time and if I'm honest I sort of wanted to pretend I wasn't turning thirty because I just felt
Feel
Felt that I hadn't done loads of the stuff that I
I mean, start a family and

Oh, you know.

I was going to ignore it, I thought that would be welcomed by my mates actually 'cause when you're my age you spend literally every weekend at a thirtieth. Or a wedding, or a baby shower, or a housewarming. Your social life is completely taken out of your hands. Anyway I said this to Holly, repeatedly, so she didn't feel compelled to book a pub function room somewhere

It got to the night before and she told me to take an overnight bag to work with me the next day

And it turned out she'd booked a weekend in Barcelona, at the W Hotel, that amazing one that's shaped like a big glass wave. So cool. Three days of sangria and tapas and sex and we Really got back to our old

It was the best thirtieth. And she made every moment of it fun and cool and I forgot about my

My

What's the male equivalent of a biological clock? Is there one? Biological... screwdriver?

Anyway.

I like your office. It's nice. Soothing. Smart. You seem to know what you're doing.

I think we can work together.

Scene Two

ADAM *is eating an M&S chicken-and-sweetcorn sandwich.*

I'm thirty-one. Same age my dad was when he left me and my mum and my little sister Ella. I thought maybe when I got to thirty-one, when I was, you know, *there*, I'd understand why he did it. I'd have empathy or something. I'd think oh yeah I'm still quite young and the idea of having kids is scary.

Nope.

I feel the opposite. I'm desperate to have kids. When I see my mates' babies I go all weird and broody. It used to freak Holly out. It freaks me out. It's quite a feminine attribute, isn't it? Shouldn't I be more into getting my dick wet or like, buying cars or punching or something

Do you want a bit of this? I'm only going to have half.

So I can't empathise with my dad. I can't understand why he did what he did. And I don't speak to him. He came crawling out of the woodwork about five years ago. He turned up at Ella's uni halls, Ella... Ella's always been a lot more... into the idea of finding him than I have. I couldn't care less. Fuck him. Don't want to exacerbate any possible daddy issues I have even further by attempting to forge an adult relationship with him. Tearful recriminations in a Caffè Nero. Throwing a ball to each other, making up for lost years. I'm alright without, thanks.

Holly would be the best mum. I think. I used to fantasise about lying in bed with her and her bump, rubbing her feet. Holly didn't exactly feel the same way. She used to make me watch *One Born Every Minute* to try and change my mind but none of it bothered me. She'd really stare me out every time the voice-over lady used the term 'mucus plug'.

Holly got pregnant for the first time when we'd been together three months. She was on the pill. It happens. She was twenty-two, I was twenty-seven, she was interning at *The Times* by day and writing for no money by night, I was still freelancing. Graphic design.

I do it for a catalogue now, full time, bit less interesting but a lot more stable, anyway that's irrelevant

It would have been insane to have had the baby.

That didn't stop me wanting it.

When she told me, over the phone, crying in a toilet stall at work, I thought – fuck it, let's just keep it.

Let's just

ADAM *takes a moment.*

I met Holly, er... four years ago. My friend Sarah had a barbecue, and the theme was the Baz Luhrmann film *Romeo + Juliet*? The one with Leo DiCaprio and Claire Danes? When you got to the barbecue, you drew a character out of a hat, and then you were handed the corresponding mask for that character... Sarah is mental. Anyway I'm sure you can guess what happened. Holly got Juliet, and I got... Quindon Tarver, the little boy who sings the cover of 'When Doves Cry'. I was one of the last to arrive. I held up my mask and this girl, this kind of striking brunette girl wearing a green dress and waving her Juliet mask around like a wand, she started pissing herself. She went, sing the song!

And I had to sing 'When Doves Cry' in the style of that little boy, because she'd said it in front of everyone and I'd have looked like a tosser if I didn't
So I sang it
I really went for it
And she was dying laughing, and she came up and grabbed my wrist and said thank you like I'd given her a really amazing present.

And she smelt like sun cream and grass and fags and she was fucking hilarious and she ate so much food. Other girls there were picking at salad and every time I saw her she had a burger or a sausage in her hand, she didn't have that social-anxiety thing loads of girls get about eating in public
And there was this inflatable flamingo in the corner, a really big, obnoxiously big inflatable flamingo, and Sarah told me that Holly had brought that with her.
Which was just
Funny.
And weird.
And six beers later I was desperate to shag her.
I could lie and say 'six beers later I was desperate to get into a committed relationship with her'
But
No, I wanted to shag her. She was – is – so fit. She's got this soft, chocolate-coloured hair that sort of rolls past her shoulders like a fucking painting or something. And her body is like, I mean, I don't want to be, let's just say she

Anyway, it got later and I managed to sit next to her as she rolled a cigarette and I asked if I could have one and dropped all the tobacco in my lap and she laughed and rolled one for me

And two hours later we were in my bedroom, and her green dress was up around her waist, and she tugged her knickers off so hard that they pinged off her ankle and into my face, and I didn't have time to find that hilarious because she
Was

The next morning was weird, I'm not great at that bit. I like to be on my own, have a think. She left and she seemed annoyed. I texted her saying that I'd had a good night. She replied saying her too, we should have a drink next week. I didn't reply, because... that's what you do.

And two days later she called me.
Why do men do this? Do you think because you've fucked me a spell has been broken? Why aren't you texting me back? It's so boring. It's predictable and boring. I'm fucking great. You should get that into your head. I'm great. I'm giving you one more chance. Okay?
And she hung up.

Anyone else, mate, anyone else, that would have sent me running for the hills.

But
Two days later we had our first proper date. I took her to a Greek place in Primrose Hill that I love. We shared a mezze and she wrapped her ankle around my calf under the table. She told me about her parents and her sister and growing up in Warwick. She made me laugh more than I'd like to on a first date, it ruined my composure, you know, the first-date veneer of cool. And you know, I can't tell you what happened next, which date was next, what the next step was because from then on was

We were just in love and it was fluid and easy and we were the smuggest couple in London, walking through Sunday sunshine with that look, that aura, that says we are happy and perfect and impenetrable.

And then we got pregnant.

Holly said she hadn't gone to Cambridge University to become a mum at twenty-two.

I went to Roehampton. Not the same is it. Still

She wouldn't even let me go with her to the
Her sister took her instead

So on a wet Wednesday morning in November I sat at the desk in my bedroom while, a couple of miles away, Holly removed our mistake, two fingers pinching a lit candle – extinguished.

I got over it. There was no other option. And I loved Holly. I *love* Holly. You don't stop loving someone like her. The love changes, it bends to move past obstacles, it becomes more or less easy and more or less pleasurable but it doesn't go away.

And even then I looked at the behaviour of my father and marvelled at his lack of gratitude, his unacceptable response to what is such a
Such a gift

Scene Three

ADAM *is on his phone.*

But my card is linked to the account

…

I see

…

Yes but the person who
Mm-hmm
Mmm
But
But the person with the
The person

…

No, yeah, it's
Surely
Surely you've had this situation before

…

No
That's not an option.

…

Yes.
And when will that be?
Fine. Okay. Thanks.

He hangs up the phone.

Sorry about that

I'm having a Netflix issue
I'm still paying for mine and Holly's Netflix account but I don't have the password.
So I can't watch it.
It's a very modern break-up problem.

I've asked her to change it to her card details, I mean I don't have her new number and she's blocked me most places but I still have her on LinkedIn so I had to ask her on there which was weird

She didn't reply

You never think you'll have to resort to messaging someone who's seen you cry during sex on LinkedIn

It's so pointedly impersonal, I mean it's the sort of thing she'd find funny
Maybe she did

That's alright, isn't it? Messaging her on LinkedIn? Or do you...?

Crying during sex wasn't a regular thing, by the way. Just something that happens when you've been together for a while and you get that need to be intimate and connect with each other even after some bad news or whatever. It's kind of pathetic but it's also an indicator of how the relationship is doing. If someone doesn't mind you getting actual tears on them mid-penetration then they're probably in it for the long haul.

I suppose I wasn't great at explaining how I felt or telling her I was sad. Sort of the way I was brought up. After my dad left my mum just wouldn't mention him. She's quite cold, my mum. We're not a close family. I mean, me and Ella are, were, well I always try with her, but she can be really
We're not a tight family unit. Unlike Holly's family, who are all harmonious and love each other and stuff, which I find disconcerting. When you go to their house everyone's happy to see each other. Nobody's bitchy or nagging or
I used to love going to Holly's for Christmas because it was like being in a film, a nice film, or a John Lewis advert.

We started doing things like Christmas and stuff like that together pretty quickly, I think because we moved in together after a year. Which was great, I loved having her then, but

She liked the flat, she liked living with me, but she didn't like
the fact that she couldn't put much money in
She was still an intern, unpaid, writing anything in the evenings
– copy for websites, speeches for people, literally anything –
and tutoring kids at the weekend. She was barely scraping by,
and she'd been at *The Times* for over a year with no full-time
job in sight. And her mate worked for this magazine, and she'd
always say Holly could work for them for a bit, just for a bit,
and Holly would tell her to fuck off, but then one Saturday I
was repainting the living room – we'd just moved in – and
Holly came in and sat down, and said

Melissa offered me another job.

And I took it.
Her face was a picture of disappointment.

And
I was pleased.
Is that wrong? I wanted her to be successful. I wanted her to
shake free of the shackles of her prosecco socialism and enjoy
herself. Be happy. Get paid.
She wanted me to say, Holly no, those magazines are
disgusting, you'll be supporting the patriarchy, think of the
refugees!
But I didn't.
I said I thought she'd made a sensible decision and she could
just do it for a couple of years.

Of course, now, now I wish she'd never
Obviously
God
I just wanted everybody to be happy

I think I'm more caring than people expect me to be. My sister
Ella thinks I'm some kind of lads'-mag-reading arsehole,
always accusing me of some slight against her or her mates or
even my own girlfriends, like she assumes all men are out to get
her. Or maybe it's just how I come across. Even Neil expressed
surprise the other day when I said I'd never cheated on anyone.
Because I haven't.
On Holly
Or anyone. Anyone ever

About two years into my relationship with Holly, I started working at the catalogue. Like I said. Good money, nice and stable. Not as cool as some of the stuff I'd done, but

Quite soon after, one of the buyers had an intern in, this eighteen-year-old girl who looked a bit like Jennifer Lawrence, and one night she kissed my neck. Right *here*.

It was weird, rather than sexy.

We were both working really late, like 11 p.m. or something – come to think of it, I suppose she was just pretending to work – and she came over with a beer for me that she'd got from the Tescos round the corner, and then she watched me work for a bit, then she bent over me and kissed my neck
And then she looked at me and I think that was when I was meant to throw her onto the desk and rip off her pants and in another world I would have but I just stared at her
Then I shook my head
And she got her coat and left.
And I said: have a nice weekend!
It was the most awkward couple of minutes of my life.
I told Holly about it, and she laughed and said she thought it was funny, but when she saw the girl at the Christmas party she 'accidentally' brushed her lit cigarette against her bare arm.

It was striking sometimes, this distance between open, honest Holly and secretive, closed-off Holly. Like this situation with Fake Jennifer Lawrence. She was obviously upset about it, and I had absolutely no idea until she'd burnt a little bit of skin off a girl's arm.

You don't know anyone. You don't actually know their thoughts and feelings, there's no way you ever will. And yet we move in with people and let them find out our deepest secrets and PIN numbers. We don't know them. Your skinny blonde fiancée could have murdered a man and tossed the body in the Thames.

Sorry. Making assumptions.

You might have a large husband and four kids. What do I know?

You're definitely not single though. Men like us…

I'm very bitter about being forced onto Tinder.

Tinder is a lot for me to take in. It became a thing when I was still with Holly. Now that I'm single I feel like I have to be on it but the experience is unpleasant. My flatmate Neil swears by it, but he definitely needs that kind of platform because he's unattractive.

The constant struggle about how to present yourself – do you use the topless Ibiza picture from when you were really toned or not – what the fuck do you write as the bio – why do you have to put your height? I'm five-eleven and that little five pisses me off. I mean what's the difference, really, between five-eleven and six? One inch, is the answer, but what I mean is girls really like there to be a six in there. So I've left mine out, but now I worry that people will think I'm freakishly short and hiding it.

She cheated, you know.
Holly.
She cheated on me.

I may seem the type but it was her, who

Ultimately

My girlfriend from school cheated on me as well. Rosie Jamieson. We were that annoying golden couple. We were too cool to be head boy and girl but we were both voted rear of the year twice in a row. My school was weird.
Anyway we were great together. Her dad was American and that made her ridiculously exotic, she ate cool cereal like Lucky Charms for breakfast which blew everyone's minds, and she always went to LA in the school holidays. LA! She was effortlessly popular. I'd had to work a bit harder, put the hours in, get good at football and finger just enough girls at parties to seem like a sexy playboy but not a scumbag. Rosie and I were the teenage dream. We lost our virginities to each other in her parents' bed one night when they were away, and the next day we walked around school in a daze, ridiculously amazed and impressed by what we'd done. We went to the leavers' dance – it's not a prom, this is England – we went to the leavers' dance in perfectly coordinated black and white. Like Justin and Britney. And like Justin and Britney, it wasn't perfect – Rosie was actually cripplingly boring, and we had basically nothing in common – but we looked so *good*.

Then the night before my Spanish GCSE Rosie called me and told me she'd been shagging one of the teaching assistants. Not even one of my peers, an actual adult, risking imprisonment and unemployment for quickies in the disabled loo. I couldn't compete with that kind of romance. When people asked why we'd broken up, I said – 'exams and that'. Which everyone accepted.

I could have got that teaching assistant fired and worse. But I didn't. It's not like I loved her.

But Holly
Holly was

Can I smoke out of your window?

Scene Four

ADAM *is flicking a lighter on and off.*

Thanks for that

I am quitting
I only started because of Holly
She made it look so cool
I think it makes me look a bit dodgy

I don't know how to quit though
I considered getting a vape, but is it ever possible to use a vape and not look like a raging twat?
I think if I can barely pull off actual cigarettes, I've got very little hope with vapes.

Do you do that thing, where every day, you get dressed with the possibility of bumping into an ex at the back of your mind?
I totally do
The other day I wanted to go and get some milk, literally five minutes down the road, and I was wearing this horrible jumper and jogging bottoms, and I opened the front door to go
And I thought hang on
I look like a disgraced PE teacher
What if Holly sees me?
Actually not just Holly

Anyone I've ever slept with
But mainly Holly

It's actually a ridiculous concern because she doesn't live here
any more. She's moved back to Warwick. With her parents.

Bit extreme.

Anyway now I only leave my house if I look good. Because I'm
a grown-up.

Holly didn't care about that. You know. Things required of an
adult

I would constantly forget that she was younger than me
By five years. Not that much, at first. Just five years. But it turns
out to be quite a gap.
I mean she was very mature. Much cleverer than me, in some
ways.

It's not even that she wanted to go out all the time, anything like
that. It's just that our timelines were a little off.

The, what I mentioned, about getting to the age with all the
wedding invites and babies and
That was just from my end. She got pissed off about it. All her
mates were still shagging around or going travelling or living
with their parents. And mine were building investment
portfolios and thinking about school districts. Not that I wanted
that, I didn't want to move to the suburbs or stop being fun, we
could have done it our way, kept our
Maybe that's naive
I was always very committed to her. And she didn't necessarily
seem as

You don't think about it though, do you. Practically. When
presented with a fit, cool twenty-two-year-old girl who thinks
you're funny and gives great head and makes you feel amazing
you don't think about, do we match up, does she want kids
young, does she think weddings are stupid
Because she did. Think weddings are stupid.
She'd wear black to them.
And roll her eyes and laugh at the wrong bits of speeches which
could be embarrassing for me
She came from such a stable, loving home. She didn't
understand the value of love. That's it, I think. She'd never

wanted for it so she didn't get how precious
Urgh, precious
But yeah, how precious it is. She didn't get it.

I'm talking about her in the past tense. I don't know why. I'm
sure she hasn't changed. I'm sure everything I'm saying about
her is still true. People don't change. They don't. I've had to
argue that point before, and it's always with someone who's
recently taken something up – like veganism or vague spirituality
or charity work, something worthy but ultimately meaningless,
and they want you to recognise that the change they've made is a
deep, visceral, soul-defining shift in personality. When actually,
doing that, jumping on a moral bandwagon like that, is just a
reflection of their existing narcissism. But they want you to watch
a video on Instagram of them doing complicated yoga poses on a
beach in India and think, wow – so-and-so has *really* changed.
That's amazing. Namaste.

When Holly took the job at the magazine, it wasn't because she
had changed. She hadn't. She was completely the same person,
but the circumstances were different. I think she probably
thought about it this way – do I stick by my principles and
refuse to work for a magazine that patronises and insults
women on a daily basis? Or do I stick by my... principles and
live in a flat that I contribute to as much as my boyfriend does?

And it took a toll on her. Working at the magazine. It was
gradual. She went into it with a sort of Blitz spirit, make the
most of the situation. She was writing for the telly section
anyway, so mainly what she did was review episodes of *The
Voice* or interview Gregg Wallace. She was kept apart from the
nasty, circles-around-cellulite bit of the business.

But, as any job does, it started taking up more of her time and
mind. She had to do a liveblog – do you know what that is? It's
like, a
She had to do a liveblog for the final of *The X Factor*, which
meant she had to be in the office, blogging for hours, because
that thing goes on for hours. I know because I was watching it
at home. Anyway she came home when it was done and she
went on this rant about it like she... like she cared. Like she
really cared. And when she noticed, she stopped, shocked at
what had come out of her mouth.
God, Adam. I sound like one of *them*.

The thing is, I would rather talk about *The X Factor* than the situation in Syria. I think almost anyone would, whether they'd admit it or not. It was easier for me. It was hard on her – at first – but it was just so easy for me. She read *Gone Girl* and quite liked it – a year before she would have completely trashed it, actually a year before she'd never have considered reading it. She came with me to a Chelsea game and only complained once. She wore a pink dress to a wedding.

I fell in love with Holly because she was complicated and difficult and interesting. But falling in love and being in a relationship require different feelings. Different qualities. So the fact that she was – I mean she was still all of those things, but – but the fact that those things were becoming less – that worked. For me. And her. It worked for us.

And if things had stayed like that forever. If she'd accepted that. If she'd kept her head down

That sounds bad

If we'd kept going like that we'd be planning a wedding right now. Instead of doing this.

That's
That's frustrating.

Scene Five

ADAM *is wearing a coat and holding a wet umbrella.*

I'm never late, this is so

Annoying

I'm never late. This is, isn't, a
I hope I didn't
You weren't waiting too long?

Pissing it down out there.

I was with my dad, actually
…
Long day. Could do without this, today. But I know

We're on a
Schedule.

Normally, of course, I'd have told him to fuck off when he got
in touch, that's what I usually do. Ella's the only one of us that
actually bothers with him. But Ella isn't answering my texts
Because she's got it into her
Female solidarity. Fucking annoying.
So I don't know, I'm tired, I'm stressed, I said yes, this was a
few weeks ago
He got in touch
I said okay fine. This is getting to be, I mean, I'm getting to be
quite

Sorry. Can I just take a minute.

…

Thanks

I wish he behaved more like a villain

He's just

Some old bloke
He's boring, if I'm honest.
He's obviously, you know, he's older and feeling guilty about
what he
Trying to make amends
All so predictable it's
It's not interesting
You want the people who have fucked with parts of your life, of
yourself, you want them to be obvious baddies. You want them
sitting on a scary armchair stroking a white cat and laughing as
servants torture babies in front of them. You at least want
sinister. Nasty. Unpleasant. Give me unpleasant, at least

He's just some boring old bloke. He drives a Volvo and he
wears jumpers from Next. He's a property surveyor. He has a
wife. They don't have children. They're members of the
National Trust.

He's just a

He took me for dinner a few weeks ago. He told me about his
life, which was fairly boring but mercifully short, and he asked

me about Holly, and my job, and it was fine. Nobody cried or
shouted, nobody threw crockery across the room. It was just so
pedestrian.

Then after that we've played squash a few times. I don't know
why, really. We haven't once mentioned the fact that he is the
man who abandoned me. I haven't asked him why he did it,
how he can live with himself, anything like that. We seem to be
pretending that we're acquaintances, like we used to work
together or something.

But today he wanted to talk. Hence being late. He wanted to
talk about

I've tolerated him so far, but my life is none of his business.
That was his choice. He can't turn up and start giving me advice
now, like he has any idea, like he's the kind of man I would
want to emulate anyway
I don't care what he thinks about
I don't
I don't require his opinion. Relationship advice from my dad
would be like getting empathy lessons from George Osbourne.
He isn't an
Appropriate

I'm sorry. This isn't my day. I'm tired. Neil dragged me out last
night to this tragic fucking singles' night organised by some
drippy girl he works with or went to school with or something.
It was utterly pathetic.

I am not the kind of man that has to go to a singles' night. I
refuse to let what's happened turn me into one of those men. I
might as well develop a bald spot and a stutter. Pathetic. I am a
proper
I am a

And the only way to cope with it was to drink, a lot, and so I
drank a lot, and ended up pulling some girl who I wouldn't be
able to pick out of a line-up now, got back late, all so fucking
depressing
It's

All so fucking depressing at the moment. Everything

Ah, I

I miss Holly. I really miss her. I miss everything about her, even the stuff I hated. I miss her body and her mouth and her hands. I miss how angry she would get if she didn't like a film we watched and I miss the way she would bite my lip when we kissed and I miss her stupid fucking Heinz jumper and god this is embarrassing
Like you give a shit
You shouldn't give a shit, it's

I just miss her, mate.

Don't you think if I just called her and
Or if I could see her

…

Never mind.

I've taken to reading old articles she wrote. Not the serious ones. The ones from the magazine. Totally vacuous stuff about series ten of *Strictly* and that reality show where the boyband Blue tried to start a nightclub in Ibiza.

If I read those articles I can hear her voice. And she's in the room with me because I can remember her telling me about writing them. So when I can't sleep I just read those

I mean that has to count for something.
You would hope.
Don't you – ?
I mean in your

She got into the swing of it, you know. At work. She started to enjoy it. She found some other imposters, other writers who couldn't give two shits about Kim Kardashian's arse workout but had ended up working there by accident, similar to her, you know. And one of them was Ashley.

Nice lad.

He had a girlfriend, Ellie? Or Emily? Or something, I did meet her, we went for dinner with them. Smug couple summit. Let's have a bottle of Pinot Noir and revel in our life choices. We went to their housewarming party as well, they were freshly moved in together, all proud of their new Le Creuset and two-bedroom shithole above a newsagent in Clapton.

Holly would say, thank God for Ashley. He's the only one who gets how stupid it all is. Someone to sit next to in meetings. Someone to get lunch with. Yeah. Thank God for Ashley.

I went on a Tinder date last week, and I only did it because the girl looked vaguely like Holly. Similar hair colour, sort of the same body, dark brown eyes like Holly's. I took this girl out for drinks and sweet-talked her into coming home with me so I could fuck her and pretend I was fucking Holly. If I squinted it was her, you know? If I covered this girl's face with a pillow it was her.

Isn't that just the
Saddest fucking thing you've ever heard.

Scene Six

ADAM *sits on the chair, silent, thinking. When he speaks, it's from nowhere.*

If office parties didn't exist, there would be a lot less infidelity.

Don't you think?

They're breeding grounds for mad behaviour. Sensible people lose their minds over cheap wine and fake Christmas trees and suddenly they're photocopying their own arsehole and fucking Dave from Accounts in the stationary cupboard.

I have a friend who used to work at an upmarket restaurant in Covent Garden. One year a big, famous company had their Christmas party there. They were loud and rowdy and didn't tip. At 3 a.m., my mate went to check the loos. Inside he found this woman, this fucking executive, passed out mid-piss. Covered in her own vomit. She must have been late forties, early fifties, power suit, seriously well-to-do woman, and she was passed out in her own sick like an eighteen-year-old fresher. Anyway he woke her up, and as she staggered out of the door, a human shit fell out of her hair. Honestly. A human turd. Most of the time that woman is probably shouting about stocks in conference calls and taking oil barons out for business lunches but because it was the office Christmas party, she became the woman with shit in her hair.

People go mad. They go mad. They must pump every office
Christmas party with some kind of airborne drug that drives
people to drink far too much and flash their tits and

Cheat on their partners.

It's the only explanation for why Holly

Alright, full disclosure. Things hadn't been fantastic. There's no
point in me lying about that. But every relationship goes
through rough patches. That's just… love. That's relationships.

I thought she'd calmed down, and when she started to exhibit
signs that maybe she hadn't, I suppose I didn't take it very well.
I mean, look at it from
For me
I thought she'd just accepted where she was. She had a good
job, Jesus, there are people who would kill for that job. She was
a working writer, even if it wasn't for the
The exact
And she had a boyfriend who adored her, and a nice house, and
attractive friends, and a good fucking life. This is what people
aspire to, isn't it? We weren't skint or fat or ill. I mean what else
What else is there?

And it seemed to me like she had mellowed, like people do as
they get older, like you're meant to, because life isn't one
massive uni common room where you can shout your feelings
about abortion and female genital mutilation all day long
You grow up
You can't make a difference. Sit down and shut up.
And you know, I wanted to get married and have kids and I
couldn't do that with her wanting to go to protests and sit-ins
and fucking gay-pride parades
And it seemed like she got that, like she'd

But
Ashley
Even his fucking name is inadequate
It only takes one person, you know, to
Ashley also hated the magazine. Ashley also wanted to write
about the important stuff. Ashley also thought he was worth
something more.

He wrote for a satirical website and one day asked Holly if she'd write something with him for it, because 'she'd said something so funny about Putin the other day' and 'she's so wasted writing for this magazine'. And she came home all excited, saying she was writing this thing with Ashley, and it was like she'd 'woken up' and she'd forgotten why she'd wanted to be a journalist, she'd been blinded by money and living comfortably – by me, was the subtext, she'd been blinded by me – and wasn't it cool that Ashley had asked her to do it?

And I said, so you're leaving a good job at a magazine that actually manages to stay in print for some blog?
No, I didn't say I was leaving anything. It's just one article.

And of course it wasn't one article, because what have I told you about Holly? She's funny and clever and talented. Ashley's editor loved her writing and then we were back, like no time had passed, to her up all night writing and reading and that buzz was back, her background noise was turned all the way up again and off she went. She'd come home and ask if I'd watched Prime Minister's Question Time? Or had I seen the thing about HSBC in the *Independent*? Or that documentary about ISIS on BBC 4? And I wanted to scream, no Holly, I haven't fucking as much as glanced at any of that stuff because I'm not interested. And you shouldn't be either. Let's go to the pub. Let's order throws from John Lewis. Let's talk about starting a family, you know that's what I want, you know that's all I want

I couldn't feign interest. I was irritated.
We were back where we started, but we had a mortgage now, you know? We had nice normal friends who didn't want to listen to her ranting on and on. We were on our way to a proper life.

She was throwing a lit match onto the warm bed that was our life. She was filling it with smoke.

I was anxious.
I mean, can you blame me?
So yes. We were arguing. We weren't really having sex. We were doing less things together.
I wanted her
To stop.

And she would scream at me, god, she would go absolutely insane at me if I tried to make my feelings known, if I tried to make her be quiet, calm down, relax.
She was exhausted and run down and up all hours. She got sick. I would hear her being sick in the mornings and late at night.
She became impossible to live with and when I tried to say that, you know, as her partner, as the person she was meant to love and be with she would

It would drive anyone to do strange things. That kind of tension, day in, day out. It would lead anyone to

I cared about her so much

Anyway
Four years we'd been together, and everything fell away in two horrible, horrible weeks, hinged on two nights that I will never forget, that she'll never forget, that
Haunt me
Is it cliched to say that? Because they do. Haunt me. They follow me around, those nights

Of course, the first night was Holly's Christmas party.
December 17th. I'd asked to go with her, isn't that what you do? She'd come with me to mine, she always came with me to mine. We were Holly and Adam. But – no, Adam you'll hate it. Everyone is such a dick, it'll be so boring, let me go alone. I won't be back late.

I prowled the flat like a caged animal that night. I felt on edge. I didn't trust
I just had a bad feeling
I
Yeah, I looked through her stuff. Laptop first. Nothing. Then I looked through her drawers and boxes and that's when
Well
I found
The pregnancy test. A tiny pink plus sign that

Pause.

She hadn't told me.

I thought maybe she was waiting to see the doctor before telling me. Something like that.

I went to bed. I felt sort of
Because she would have to slow down. She would have to give
up and relax and be with me.

Her key turned in the lock at about 3 a.m. I pretended to be
asleep. She stumbled in, pulling her tights off, falling into the
chest of drawers. She got into bed next to me. A few minutes
later she was snoring, drunk snores. Last night of boozing for a
while, I thought. I rolled over, put my arm around her.

The unmistakeable scent of aftershave that isn't yours.

I could have shaken her awake, demanded answers. Tears.
Begging forgiveness. A quickly packed bag. A slammed door.

I ignored it. She was pregnant. I had her. The aftershave hit the
back of my throat. I could taste it.

And *I'm* the bad guy.

Scene Seven

ADAM *seems animated and positive*.

Oh god, we'd absolutely been drinking yeah

Drugs too

Is that not
I thought I'd mentioned that?
Oh yeah. I mean it was New Year's Eve. It's not like either of us
are like, mad addicts or anything
I mean, I'm thirty-one, I take it easy
Or I
When we were younger, both of us, we, you know. Nothing
hardcore. Just the stuff that everyone does. And I do mean
everyone. As we got older, we did it less and less until I decided
we'd only do drugs at festivals or on New Year's. And we don't
really go to festivals any more.
So yeah, god yeah. Not a lot, but yeah. I thought I'd mentioned
that?

I mean that was the whole point, the er, the cornerstone of that

What I mean was, that was the tell. For me.

I'm not making

Basically

It was New Year's Eve. I'd found the pregnancy test two weeks before.

And things were

Holly had gone home for Christmas. I always went with her.

But she just announced she was going on her own

That I should spend time with my mum

With my *mum*, what the

And she went away on the

Must have been 20th? Something like that

Still hadn't told me about the

Hard Christmas. Hard for me. I'd call her every day, you know, and she'd be so fucking

So distant and weird

I suppose you're thinking, why didn't I say something?

Confront her about the

The truth is she had hidden it, the test, you know, it's not like I found it in the bin and I didn't want her thinking I was spying on her or anything like that and

And like I said last time, I thought she was keeping it from me for a reason and that reason would become clear

So

She came home on New Year's Eve.

We were going to a house party, Sarah's party, Sarah of *Romeo + Juliet* barbecue fame

The theme this time was Disney because as previously mentioned Sarah is fucking weird but luckily we were allowed to choose our own characters this time

I'd totally forgotten that we had to dress up, to be honest, but Holly got home on the 31st with bags of crap from her mum's house and declared that we were going as The Incredibles.

She'd got red spandex leggings and leotards. There's a picture, did I give it to you?

You have a copy, right?

Yeah

Yeah, well things had been weird, strained, I don't know, and obviously we hadn't seen each other

But she pitched up at ours all… normal. She seemed happy.

With these stupid fucking costumes
That normally I'd probably have argued about, I wasn't hugely
keen on going out in red spandex, but she seemed really, you
know

I was surprised she wanted to go out. With the baby, the
pregnancy, I.

I thought maybe she was going to tell me that night. I mean, I
would notice her not drinking

But she did drink
A lot
She did not stop drinking, actually. I was sweating in my stupid
spandex as I watched her at the party, all chatty, calm, cool, and
drinking. Vodka and soda. By the pint.
Then she went off to the loo with her mate and came back doing
the, you know, sniffing thing

I felt sick, mate. Sick.
But we were at a party, I couldn't
I just kept drinking. Kept going. But it built up and eventually I
took her aside, 1 a.m. or something, and just went – Holly, we
need to go home
We need to go home.

She was pissed and I was sort of pissed and she didn't want to
come with me but I booked an Uber and sort of shepherded her
into it
And in the car she sang along to that stupid 'Happy' song on the
radio and I got tighter and tighter inside, thinking over and over
again – she's pregnant and she's been drinking, she's pregnant
and she's been drinking, she's pregnant and she's been drinking,
until the first bit fell away – she's been drinking, she's been
drinking, she's been drinking. And it was like
Like a fog
Everything went dark and we got home and out of the taxi and
into the flat and she was still singing
Because I'm happy

She was really fucked. All over the place. I was, I don't know, I
felt drunk of course, but I was also quite

She was in our bedroom, getting changed, she was just in her
underwear

I stared at her stomach, as if I could see through the skin and the muscle and right inside

Holly
What happened to the baby?

She looked at me, a bit shocked, too drunk to cover that up, then shrugged it off
What are you on about?

Now this is where it gets a bit
I mean, it was not a nice
It was awful. For both of us. That conversation.

Anyway I sort of grabbed her, shook her, trying to wake her up, sober her up, I don't know
What happened to the baby?
And she kept saying I don't know what you mean, I don't know what you mean
So I
I grabbed her chin, like this
So I could look her right in the eyes, so she couldn't avoid me, you know, so she couldn't
And I said, something along the lines of
Tell me right now what happened or I will hurt you.
Moment-of-madness stuff. You know. I was, I'm sure you can understand, I was beside myself.
And she looked at me, finally, in the eyes, all bleary, all pissed and
And went,
Adam, I got rid of it.
I don't love you any more. We can't have a baby.

Then she pushed me off her.

Just the worst words I've ever heard.

I don't love you any more. We can't have a baby.
I got rid of it in Warwick.

This isn't working. I wasn't going to say any of this tonight but you've made me.

And then she said,
You stifle me.
She was crying.

You make me feel invisible.
I loved you and you stifled me.

She was crying and drunk and half-naked and I was crying and
drunk
And I reacted
Out of the
I just thought about the baby
I got rid of it in Warwick
I got rid of *it* in Warwick?

I deserved that baby. I deserved it. We were meant to have a
baby and be happy and normal
I hadn't worked on her for
I hadn't
I hadn't put *years* into her to

And I said, this is because of Ashley then, is it? You're fucking
him behind my back and
And she denied it, of course she denied it
Ashley's my friend, it's not like that
Yeah, yeah.
I kind of screamed at her to, you know, admit it, admit that
she'd been sneaking around with that poncey little cunt, fucking
him at work and coming home to me, but it was all wide eyes
and no, no, you're wrong

It happened really quickly, I think, and like I said we were both
drunk.

I wanted her near me and I wanted to convince her to change
her mind and I wanted to beat Ashley and I wanted our baby
and I wanted to give her another chance to go back on what
she'd done
So I pulled her onto the bed, and can I just say, she didn't tell
me to stop, she was just crying
Like I said before, sometimes couples cry during
I wanted her, it was, I don't know, but through the fog of anger
and distress I felt this huge pull towards her and I wanted to be
inside, as close, as close as I could get, as close as

She didn't say no

I don't think she said no

I probably was quite rough. I didn't notice, it wasn't intentional, but it was very emotional, and yeah I think I was probably quite rough
And she was crying
And no, I mean, in terms of 'consent' – you don't get written consent from your live-in girlfriend every time you have sex

I suppose, uh, I suppose I had her arms pinned back, maybe. But that's quite

I mean, come on. We'd been together for three years, and this was obviously an extremely difficult piece of news for me to hear, and I was upset, I was past upset, I was distraught
She had betrayed me, seriously betrayed me, and I could have done worse, I mean, you'd understand if

If I'd hit her or

I didn't hit her. I just
We just

I stopped when I saw she was bleeding. From

I
I
Obviously I'd been quite rough. Rougher than I meant to be

But, yes, it's not a nice, it wasn't a nice, I can see that, but to call it
What *she's* calling it

I mean
You can see it from my

…

I was worried about her, I mean, because of the bleeding and, and she was drunk and
But I was also extremely angry so I just
Walked out, got in the car
Don't mention that in
I mean that looks bad
I was drunk, slightly, no, very drunk, er
Very irresponsible, I'll admit, that isn't okay. But anyway I drove, to Hampstead Heath, and just sort of walked around for hours

Sobering up
Thinking about

Thinking about what she'd done to me.
She had been brutal.

And when I got home the next morning she'd left, most of her
stuff gone, and at first I was glad, you know. I didn't want to see
her or speak to her, I was furious, I was hurt, god I felt like I'd
been stabbed in the gut
So I didn't call her, that's why I didn't call her, I was just so
angry
And a week passed
And then I got the call from the police.

And here we are.

So, what do you think?

Scene Eight

ADAM *is dressed in a dark (but not black) suit. He's drinking a
bottle of San Miguel.*

I'm not like my dad. I'm resilient. I stick with things, even if
it's hard. I stick with people. I'm not going to hold it against my
mates. Or Ella. Or Holly, even. I'm going to accept apologies.

He drinks.

When I get back in the office, I'm going to celebrate by getting
a mini-fridge. Yours is great.

Cheers.

He drinks.

In a way it was a shame I didn't get to, I don't know

Explain what actually happened

It's sort of anti-climactic for it to be just based on a lack of
forensic evidence, that's what it's, forensic evidence, yeah?
Sort of saying well it could have happened but we can't prove it
I'd rather have had it kind of laid out that it just wasn't true, but

I don't want to complain
You did what was easiest, I'm not criticising, I'm just worried
that it won't reflect well on me
But it was good you mentioned that we'd been out, and she'd
been drinking, and the rest
I think it was important to point that out
I just hope that's enough to

Although, I had texts from a couple of the lads earlier, actually.
Haven't heard from them in months, but a couple have
apologised and that. Hopefully Ella will get in touch soon and
we can just get over this weird

Silly
Situation.

And everything will just

I mean I honestly think if I'd been allowed to just talk to Holly,
face to face, at some point in the last few months it wouldn't
have got this far. I think she just got caught up in the

The feelings and the

And she couldn't speak to me, so it all just got
I still miss her, I'm not angry with her, I, you know, I can see
how this got so big and messy

I still love her

You know, there have been benefits, for her. She left her job.
She hated that job. I wonder how positive a change that's been.
I wonder if she misses it
I wonder if she misses me
It just seems so harsh if she doesn't, so cold, I don't, that
doesn't seem like Holly

My reaction, what happened, is just an indication of how
strongly I felt, still feel, about her.

Like, when I told you about my girlfriend from school? And
how little I reacted when she fucked the teaching assistant? I
mean that shows, doesn't it, that I don't react badly to things in
general, I don't have any kind of

I'm not violent or

I just love her and she hurt me. It was a weird fucking evening, mate. That's all it was.

ADAM*'s phone gets a text. He reads it.*

Neil.

'Well done mate, knew it would be okay'
Yeah cheers mate
I can probably ditch him now. I know that's mean, bless him and everything. But he is a cretin.

And I want my old life back. Old mates.

…

When Ella found out, I mean
When it all came out, you know
She came over to my house
And she was crying
And she said that she wasn't surprised. Can you believe that?
She said I hated women, always had.

Couldn't be further from the truth. I love women. I was brought up by a woman. Ellie's my little sister, for
She was obviously just, I don't know, reacting to something, god knows, whatever, but it really hurt me, and I
I'm looking forward to seeing her and

I love women. After all, everything I did, depending on how you, but actually everything that happened was
I was trying to help Holly.
I was just trying to give her a good life.
From day one. Maybe not day one. From the day we sat in the Greek restaurant, I thought – I want to look after you. I want to make you mine.

How anyone can see that as hate, is

Can I smoke out of your window?

Blackout.

End.

PRIMADONNA

Rosie Kellett

*For my family,
and their unwavering support.*

Rosie Kellett was accepted into Soho Theatre's Writer's Lab 2015/16.

Rosie's writing credits include *Skint*, developed with the support of the
National Theatre Young Studio, supported by the Paul Hamlyn Foundation
(VAULT Festival 2015, winner of the Pick of the Week and Festival Spirit
Awards); *Morker* (Southwark Playhouse, developed on the Almeida Theatre's
Writers' Development Programme); and *Peak* (Old Red Lion Theatre).

Acknowledgements

Huge thanks and love to Jamie Jackson for his endless dramaturgical support, without whom, I would be lost at sea.

Many thanks to the National Youth Theatre, God's Own Junkyard, Tim Wilson, Mat Burt, Andy George, Charlie Weedon, Jake Ogden, Sian O'Gorman, Oliver Byng, Anna Piper, Craig Talbot, Alex Rand, Paul Spraggon, Phao May, Lauren Bevan, Ros Wyatt and James Vernon.

R.K.

Primadonna was first performed at VAULT Festival, London, on 17 February 2016, with the following cast:

ROSIE	Rosie Kellett

Director	Jamie Jackson
Producer	Desara Bosnja
Technical Manager and Operator	Remi Smith
Assistant Producer	Lily Staff

Characters

ROSIE
LUCY
MARNI
CRESSY
WREN
AD
JENNIFER AT JOHN LEWIS CUSTOMER SERVICES
MUM
TIMMY

Note on Text

In the original production, all the characters were played by one actor. In future productions, other characters can be played by other actors if necessary.

The references to the original production (and director) can be adapted/taken out as needed.

Introduction

ROSIE *is on stage building a bed, she has all the parts laid out, the instructions and tools. As the audience arrive, she assembles the bed as best she can, just before the show starts it should be finished apart from one leg which is missing. She searches for the missing leg until it's time for the show to start.*

The show will start with one leg still missing and the bed half-standing up. Adele's rare songs/covers/B-sides are playing, not everyone should realise it's Adele.

House lights go down, spotlight up on ROSIE *who steps centre stage.*

Music fades down.

ROSIE   Thanks Adele.
           Hi
           My name is Rosie
           I have ginger hair.
           It's not real, although my dad is ginger and he was in Simply Red.
           He's not Mick Hucknall.
           I have three siblings.
           I am the least special.
           Lola is the oldest.
           Isla is the youngest.
           And Jack is the only boy.
           He's also the only one of us that's annually got away with giving us a photo of our dog for Christmas.
           Until 2013 when we put our foot down.
           Everything in this story is based on truth.
           It all happened in mine or Jamie's actual lives.
           We have decided to change some of the names and places
           But that was the only piece of advice my dad's lawyer gave us
           In exchange for a cheese-and-ham croissant
           So, cheers Paul.

I go to the theatre at least once a week
And I hate myself for just saying that
But I also hate audience participation.
With a vicious passion.
So I want you to understand
If I ask for your help
It's literally because I can't tell the story on my own.
I'm telling it on my own because there isn't enough
Rescue Remedy in the UK to get Jamie through a
job interview
Let alone six shows at VAULT Festival
So, thanks.

1.

ROSIE   This might surprise you
But I was not in the popular group as a child
I know
This confident adult you see before you was not
cool in school
I mean I don't think it was my fault; there was a lot
against me
My dad was in a band
And we lived in the 'big house'
So naturally I was 'the posh bitch'
In Year 7 there was a school trip to my village and
our house was used as an example because of its
historical relevance
And you know
All the boys spat on our front door.
I wasn't allowed a Tamagotchi
So I made one out of cardboard
Which everybody laughed at
But, you know, joke's on them
Because it's still alive
In my imagination.
When everyone else was singing along to the Spice
Girls and celebrating girl power

I was listening to David Gray in the back of my
dad's car on the way to orchestra rehearsal.
We weren't really allowed to watch TV
Unless it was our VHS copy of *Little Women*
So I never knew what was going on in *Neighbours*
And to this day I blame that for my inability to do
an Australian accent.
Thanks Mum.
To add insult to injury
I was also a mini-version of my mother
I loved to make a list
Lists were my best friends, quite literally
I was super-organised and some might say bossy.
So in an effort to survive the rural state-school
system
I became a pleaser and spent my childhood finding
ways to fit in
Working out what my classmates were thinking
What they thought was cool
And just pretending I did too
I mean sure
I didn't like Katy Perry and I still don't
But I went to the Teenage Dreams tour with a smile
on my face and bought a T-shirt for forty pounds
And although all that caused me a great deal of
hassle and unhappiness at school;
My desire to please,
Organisational skills,
And knowledge of plant-based diets,
Has made me
The perfect PA.

2.

ROSIE   I met Lucy in a strange way
            We live near each other
            And went to a lot of the same places
            I think I first recognised her in yoga
            And then at the market
            Then in a coffee shop
            And it was just one of those things
            Eventually we got talking
            She told me she was a producer
            I thought she was my age
            Turns out she has a deceptively youthful appearance
            But I think it was my bag or something

            She was all like

            'Oh my god sorry but where is this from, I think
            my best friend Tabitha makes these'

            And it turns out Tabitha had made my bag
            Then we realised we go to all the same places
            Have the same hairdresser

            'Oh no we love Ricardo, I've been seeing him
            since I was twelve'

            And drink at the same pub

            'Ahm, they do my favourite Scotch eggs and their
            craft beer is actually really good'

            It was weird for me because I hadn't lived here for
            long and hadn't really made any friends
            Most people just kept themselves to themselves
            It takes time to make friends in London
            And it's understandable to be protective of that
            But she was the first person I'd really made friends
            with
            Or at least
            I don't know if you'd call it friends
            But it was lovely to have someone who knew my
            name
            Who I could wave at in the park
            And sit next to in yoga.

Turns out, we aren't that similar and I have my
own friends now
But looking back,
If you told me
That in a year's time
I would have spent more time at her house than at
my own
And that I would know details about her
That even she didn't know
And that I would forget things about myself
And who I am
And that in amongst all that
I would feel lonelier than I have ever felt

If you told me that then
I'd have told you to fuck off.

3.

*We're in Shoreditch House, there is thumping dance music
playing.*

LUCY *is sitting on a sofa, pouring herself a glass of wine.* [*In
the original production,* TIMMY *was represented by a balloon
tied to the other side of the sofa at head-height.*] *Music fades to
a low level.*

LUCY Oh Rosie hi
    Over here sweetie
    Timmy Rosie
    Rosie Timmy
    Soooo good to see you
    Isn't it good to see her Timmy?
    How are you?
    Brilliant okay

    Yes no very good
    We got back yesterday didn't we Timmy
    No I mean it was perfect
    Obviously
    You know I was too stressed to enjoy it of course

Didn't eat for days
But Timmy had a great time
Didn't you Timmy
I mean it was crazy
Everyone was so drunk
And oh Timmy you tell her
No go on you tell
Okay no I will.
Timmy's friend Wex,
Wex spiked Timmy's drink with LSD and then I
drank it by accident
And there I was tripping on acid!
I mean it was hilarious
Only I did fuck up the certificate
Everyone was off their tits
Timmy you were off your tits
Weren't you Timmy?
Sorry Rosie what was the question?
Yes no our wedding, no really great.

So you've brought your CV
Thanks sweetie
Timmy where are my glasses?
Did you forget them?
Oh Timmy
You're useless
He's useless.

LUCY *is holding the CV away from her face trying to read it, she can't without her glasses.*

Well CVs aren't really on-brand for me anyway
I'm more interested in people's vibes than the jobs
they've done before meeting me.

LUCY *rips up the CV.*

So maybe you could describe your vibe to me in a
few words?

ROSIE   My vibe?
I'm sorry I don't really understand
Could you –
What exactly do you mean?

LUCY   Okay no sure
              So currently my team is made up of girls with vibes
              that really complement each other
              Cressy's vibe is that she's super-creative with
              budget and always manages to make things
              beautiful super-cheaply.
              Ahm Marni's vibe is that she's the intern,
              And of course my vibe is that I'm super-organised
              and super-busy
              So how do you think your vibe could complement
              and fit in with the rest of the team's?

ROSIE   Okay
              Um they all sound like they've got great vibes
              Mine I guess is more
              Well I suppose my vibe would be kind of –
              I'm really organised

LUCY   No that's my vibe.

ROSIE   Sorry
              Okay um well I'm really good at working well
              under pressure
              And being on time
              And also included in my vibe is –
              I make a great cup of tea

LUCY   I actually only drink Nespresso.

              Okay okay Rosie
              Cool
              Interesting
              Yah so the thing is
              My brain's full
              Isn't it Timmy?
              And we're just so busy aren't we Timmy?
              I'm swamped at work at the moment you know
              We've got things in pre-production, filming and in
              post all at the same time
              And poor Timmy is run off his feet
              So we need someone who can just
              Be our brain
              You know
              Make sure we have food in the house

Organise our travel
Look after our property
And sometimes I'll need you more and then other
times Timmy will need you won't you Timmy?
So it will just depend on what's going on and who
needs you more you know
One day you could be on set with me
The next you could be flying to Bali with Timmy
But I guess –
Oh no Timmy go on
Were you going to say something?
No okay
Well I was just going to say
We're really fun
Aren't we Timmy?
And we want you to have fun working with us you
know
And hopefully you can learn something from us
you know
And it's not all work and no play
We have the summer social of course when we all
go to Glastonbury
And we like to treat you all occasionally don't we
Timmy?
I mean for example
This year we took the girls to a jelly-sculpting class
It was really immersive
We work hard but we play even harder don't we
Timmy?

Okay great, well I guess we should order an Uber
then Rosie and head back to the office
Got to start blending your vibe with the rest of the
team
Timmy can you please get a haircut today
I won't take you away at the weekend until you've
had a haircut
Don't you think he needs a haircut Rosie?

ROSIE   Um welll –

LUCY   Exactly
Now off you go bubsy

Love you
Do you love me?
Bubsy do you love me too?
Good now off you go
Straight to the hairdressers'.

4.

We're in LUCY*'s office. There is a swivel chair and a desktop*
keyboard that sits on the actor's lap while they are on the chair.
[In the original production, the swivel chair moved each time
the character changed to represent where they sat in the office.]
MARNI *is 'Valley Girl' American and* CRESSY *is posh British.*

MARNI   And then I was like really?
           You know I have a lot of issues around Chipotle
           and you're gonna say that to me?
           Like what an A-hole.

CRESSY   Yah totally.
           He's such an arsehole.
           You really should drop that like a hot potato and
           run a mile Marn.

MARNI   I feel like he doesn't respect my energy
           He doesn't respect my passions
           And he isn't even committed to my chakra

CRESSY   No.
           Fuck that shit.

MARNI   Like if I want to bless the energy above our bed
           before we make love
           I should be able to do that.
           He just needs to practise patience
           You know?

CRESSY   Absofuckinglutely.
           Whilst we're on that, can you give me an update on
           our Christmas social.
           Are we doing the reiki healing workshop or the
           sound bath?

MARNI   Okay
            So I'm pushing to do both because I feel like a
            sound bath is the ultimate way to follow a reiki
            healing workshop
            But Lucy is like only gonna pay for one
            Cos she and Timmy have got this new assistant or
            whatever
            And apparently we have to include her or
            something

CRESSY   Oh
            That's disappointing
            Why does she have to come
            She's new

MARNI   I know they are my exact same feelings
            But like she's already invited her or whatever

CRESSY   Ugh that's really inconvenient for me,
            I've been looking forward to that sound bath since
            Glastonbury

MARNI   I know right she sounds awful

ROSIE   Sorry is this Lucy's office?

CRESSY   Who's asking?

ROSIE   Sorry
            Rosie
            Hi
            I'm Lucy and Timmy's new assistant

MARNI   Oh my god Rosa
            Come in
            Make yourself comfortable
            So great to meet you
            Welcome
            How are you?

ROSIE   Great thanks, it's Rosie, lovely to meet you

CRESSY   (*Clearly not impressed by* ROSIE.)
            Oh Rosa
            Hi
            We're so glad to have you on board

MARNI   Yah we're like so excited to have you here or
             whatever
             Let me give you the tour
             So over there we have the creative pod where we
             have our weekly brain dump and sometimes we
             have our morning meditation in there too
             Then in the corner we have the juice bar
             That's just a help-yourself kinda thing
             And the yoga studio is downstairs
             Joss runs classes daily at 7 a.m.
             She's a gentle soul and a really grateful yogi so
             don't miss out
             Let me or Cressy know if you have any questions
             whatsoever
             Right Cress?

CRESSY   Yeah, ask me anything
             As long as I'm not on the phone, or talking to
             Marn, or looking at my laptop, or texting.
             Otherwise, fire away.
             I should probably say we also don't really allow
             food at the desk space so if you are going to eat
             that falafel, please eat it outside
             Juice is fine.

             I sit next to Lucy,
             Marni sits next to me,
             And there's no room next to Marni,
             So you can have the spare desk.

ROSIE   Okay thanks
             I'll just –
             Where should I put this –

MARNI   Oh the ukulele is mine
             And that coconut water should be in the fridge
             But you can just dump the box of slinkys
             somewhere else.

             Lights down.

5.

ROSIE   Things Lucy has said to me in the last twenty-nine minutes…

Rosie did you order the lip sofa?
Rosie did you find a non-homogenised-milk supplier?
Rosie did you fish this water out of the Thames? It's foul.
Rosie have you dealt with the glitter balls?
Rosie are you aware all the office plants are dying?
Rosie you look like death
Rosie what's that smell?
Oh it's your perfume.
Rosie my phone's broken
Rosie I need a sexy Hallowe'en costume
Rosie we need a second office Nutribullet
Rosie I'm worried about you but also where's my coffee?
Okay no I don't want it any more.

6.

We're back at Shoreditch House with LUCY *and* ROSIE. *They are having a meeting and waiting for* WREN *to arrive.*

LUCY   Okay and where are we with the restaurant for tomorrow?

ROSIE   So we have a few options, I have four places that are within walking distance from the hotel, they all have vegan options but also several red meat options.

LUCY   Let me see?

ROSIE *hands* LUCY *an iPad.*

No, we need somewhere bigger,
I've been to all those places and none of them are big enough.

ROSIE   Well this one has a capacity of two hundred; it's set
           over two floors and has three menus to choose
           from –

LUCY   No I don't think you understand, Rosie.
           When I say this is a big client,
           What I mean is he is a large client,
           He isn't small,
           He is big,
           What I'm saying is we need to find somewhere
           with booth seating.

ROSIE   Oh I see so it's not the size of the restaurant?

LUCY   No! God I thought I made that quite clear, we just
           need to find somewhere within a four-minute walk
           from his hotel, that has booth seating and a vegan
           option for his wife and lots of meat options for him.
           I'm not asking for the moon here.

ROSIE   No okay well that's clear now.

LUCY   So we ended up casting Wren Baker as the hero girl
           in next week's commercial.
           Last-minute success thanks to me!
           She'll be here any minute.
           Her agent's just got in touch,
           We need to get her a green juice before she arrives
           and make sure we're sitting near a window but also
           away from the light.
           Can you sort that out?
           Great.

ROSIE   (*Breaking character.*)
           Again, this is where Paul, my dad's lawyer, suggests
           I change the names of a few key characters,
           All for a pastry that cost more than your ticket
           tonight.
           Wren wasn't even his idea,
           That was all me,
           I could be a lawyer.

LUCY   I think this chat will really just be to put her mind
           at rest you know assure her that we are here for her
           and that there's nothing to worry about.

She's very busy,
In super-high demand,
We're very lucky to have got her.
So we need to make her feel welcome
And appreciated
And like we're on her side et cetera et cetera
You've seen her work right?

ROSIE   Um sorry what was her name?

LUCY   Wren.
Wren Baker.

ROSIE   Oh no I'm not sure
I would probably recognise her face –

LUCY   Oh give me strength –
Come on Rosie!
You seriously don't know who she is?
You would recognise her.
She has one of those faces.
But she's also a really big fucking deal in the
industry.
Very highly respected.
She's like Joaquin Phoenix you know –
Crazy,
Slightly strange-looking.
But incredibly talented.
She's like a female Joaquin Phoenix.
Fucking nightmare, she'll drive you crazy but it's
worth working with her for the kudos you know.

WREN *arrives*.

Wren sweetie darling!
Sooooo good to see you.

ROSIE   Hi
Rosie
Lovely to meet you

LUCY   We got you a juice or something
Green juice
Didn't we Rosie?
Oh bring that over here.

Yes green juice –
Over here now.

WREN *sits down.*

WREN   Oh no I don't need a green juice.
Very sweet of you,
But I'm fine,
Thanks.

LUCY   No sure absolutely
Quite right.

LUCY *throws the juice over her shoulder.*

So Wren this is Rosie, she's mine and Timmy's
assistant but she'll be working on the shoot pretty
much full time.
She'll be in charge of your accommodation and
travel,
Won't you Rosie?

ROSIE   Yeah for sure
Just let me know if there's anything specific you
need and –

WREN   Right –
Sorry.
I'm a bit confused –

LUCY   No not at all,
What's the problem?
I'm sure we can sort it.

WREN   Well it's Rosie right?
Sorry.
You're Lucy's assistant?

LUCY   Yes that's right mine and Timmy's
My husband
Timmy
We share her

WREN   Okay.
Sorry.
I'm just a bit confused as to why

Rosie,
You'll be helping me with my shelter.
Such personal issues –
That's something my assistant should be doing.
Sorry –
I'm just a very private person.
I have my babies to look after.
Have they not started yet?
Are they going to be joining us today?

LUCY   Who?

WREN   My assistant?
When are they arriving?
You've got me an assistant right?

LUCY   Yeah –
I mean –
Well –
Yah –
I mean.

           LUCY *is looking around, mostly at* ROSIE, *it
           becomes clear that she means her.*

WREN   Sorry is there a problem?

LUCY   No not at all.
Well I mean –
Rosie
That's what –

ROSIE   Sorry?
Me?

LUCY   Well I mean you're here to assist me.
And I'm here to make sure Wren has everything
She needs
So basically,
That's basically,
It's totally doable,
Is what I'm saying.
As long as that's cool with you Wren?

WREN   Yeah I mean –
I suppose I don't mind, giving you a chance,

I have quite specific needs
What with my babies,
And with the way I work.
My process is quite unique.
I'll need absolute commitment from you,
But as long as nothing is compromised
And I have everything I need,
I suppose I don't mind.

LUCY   Wow.
          Rosie!
          Lucky you.
          What a great opportunity for you!

ROSIE   Right –
          Yeah no.
          Thanks.

WREN   You're welcome.
          I guess for me it's mostly help with my food and
          the odd errand
          I should probably just quickly bring you up to date
          with my dietary,
          I'm having some tests done at the moment to work
          out what my allergies are –
          Yeah I have a lot.
          So my nutritionalist is cutting out a few areas to try
          and narrow it down.
          But it's basically limited to
          No meat
          No fish
          No dairy

ROSIE   Okay so basically vegan?

WREN   No gluten
          No sugar
          No yeast

ROSIE   Right are you coeliac? –

WREN   No egg white
          No peanuts
          No walnuts

No sesame seeds
No white cabbage
No red cabbage
No avocado
No olive oil
No coconut oil
No canola oil
No dark soy sauce
No beans

ROSIE   When you say beans –

WREN   No lentils
No brown rice
No white rice
No black tea
No egg noodles
No mussels
No oysters
No white potato
No vegetable oils
No coffee
No figs
No oats
No grapefruit
No orange
No yogurt
No milk powder
No margarine
No lactose
No kiwi
No banana
No prawns
No spelt
No rye
No quinoa
No almonds
No red pepper
No strawberry

And I think that's it at the moment.

ROSIE   Right
           Okay
           Do you have any example meals that we can start
           with?

WREN   No.
           Oh and I also have asthma, sensitive skin and a
           mild vertigo.

           It's also important for me to have all my tools with
           me on set.
           Just as carpenter would have his tool bag,
           I too have tools I use to help me feel comfortable
           and get me where I need to be.

ROSIE   Sure.
           Do you know what you might need and I can make
           sure we have it for our first day shooting?
           Do you have a list that we could –

WREN   Sweetie.
           What you'll learn about me
           Is that I can't always predict
           What I'm going to need.
           I will need all the obvious things –
           My headphones,
           My music,
           Tissues,
           Tiger Balm,
           Lavender oil,
           My inhaler,
           Fiji water.

           It's obvious stuff,
           But we haven't worked together before
           So I won't expect you to pick all this up
           immediately.
           We can just see how it goes
           And work things out as we go –
           It'll be fun!

7.

It's shoot day.

Music plays. [In the original production, ROSIE picked members of the audience to play the AD and camera operator.]

AD	Okay we're going to go for another one. Everyone ready? Checks happy? Rosie, are we good to go? Rosie?
	ROSIE *is standing with* WREN.
ROSIE	Okay, so Wren I think they're ready for another take, it's just going to be the same close-up again of you –
WREN	I need my headphones –
ROSIE	Well I think they're ready to go now –
WREN	Well I'm not. They're going to have to wait for me aren't they?
AD	Okay we're ready to go. Quiet on set please.
WREN	I'm not ready yet Rosie –
ROSIE	We just need a few more minutes please –
WREN	Where's the set bag? Where's my cacao? Where did we put it? We need to find it.
ROSIE	Okay um okay –
WREN	Look it's under my chair Rosie – Bring it here. Chop chop! I need my cacao, Look it's under my chair. Bring it here quickly, And my headphones. Get my headphones out

And put the song on,
Quickly,
They're waiting
And a tissue.

I need a lozenge,
Hairspray,
Now!
Hurry up,
Inhaler,
Tiger Balm,
I need the Tiger Balm,
Rub it here.
Hurry up.
Tissue.
Quickly.
Water.
Pass me the water.

AD   Okay Rosie we really need to squeeze one last take
in before lunch.
Are we all ready?

WREN   No we're not ready you're going to have to hold on!
Okay take it away.
Too late.
You're too slow.

WREN *is pacing up and down, breathing heavily,
rubbing her hands together and jumping on the
spot.*

Okay

WREN *sits down for the take.*

Well I'm ready

[*In the original production, an audience member
was given a window frame and watering can, and
instructed to hold the frame in front of* WREN's
face.]

AD   Okay thank you.
Quiet on set please?

Sound speed.
And we're rolling.
And action.

WREN *stays seated.* [*The audience member pours water from the watering can in front of the window frame like rain.*]

WREN *stays there for a matter of seconds.*

And cut.
Thank you boys and girls, that's lunch.
I make it two-fifteen, back on set at three-fifteen please.

8.

ROSIE   So I'm getting Wren's lunch from Wagamama's.

LUCY   She can't do that.

WREN   I can.

LUCY   Okay no we love Waga's.
          Get me a chilli greens.

ROSIE   (*On phone.*) Hi
          Good thanks
          How are you?
          Great
          Okay
          Sorry I have a bit of a nightmare order.
          Yeah can I just ask you a few questions?
          Do you handle meat and fish in the same area that you handle vegetables?
          Sure
          And do you have different chefs for the vegetarian foods?
          Like chefs for the meat and fish foods
          And then an entirely different human being for the vegetarian food?
          I've just been asked to –

Sorry I know this is a bit weird
Okay another question, is your soy sauce light and
is it organic?
Do you think you can tell when you taste it?
That it's not organic?
If I just tell someone it is?
Do you think she'll be able to tell from tasting it?
And just so I have some more info, what brand
would it be if it was organic?
Okay. Sorry.
I can google that.
So then I'd like to order a number four,
But could I please ask that you use green chilli
rather than red
And that you put the garlic in the oil when it's
cold?
Sorry it's not for me.
I know but she'll be able to tell if you put it in
when it's hot.
Sorry.
She just will.
Thanks.
Okay great.
And I know this is a bit weird
But if I tell you the things she can eat, can you try
and make something out of them maybe?
Just something simple?
Okay amazing.
So they all need to be organic, but she can eat:

Wasabi
Soy
Kale
Black sesame seeds
And vegetable broth

No that's it.
She just wants something simple and clean
Reckon you could whip a little something up?

9.

ROSIE   So Lucy,
          Just a quick one –
          Yeah,
          So Wren's bed,
          She isn't happy with the fibres,
          Or in fact,
          Any of it.
          She says it feels cheap
          And that –
          Her words, not mine –
          I'm just repeating what she said to me –
          That it's made from synthetic fibres and that she
          may as well be sleeping in a bin bag on the carpet.
          Right.
          Yeah.
          She also said –
          Do you want to hear it?
          She did ask me to tell you all this so I think I should.
          She said that she could inhale the contents of the
          hoover bag and –
          Yeah I know that but –
          And lie on a bed of rusty nails –
          And have a better night's sleep.
          I'm sorry.
          I just had to pass it on.
          She made me promise.
          She'd know.
          If I hadn't.
          She just would.

LUCY   Well we're not putting her in a hotel if that's what
          you're getting at.
          There isn't the budget.
          Get her a new bed.
          I have that delivery thing,
          Use the black card and order it on that website I like.
          Get it to come by lunchtime,
          But I don't want to pay extra for the delivery.

ROSIE   Okay Luc–

          We hear the sound of a phone being hung up.

10.

JL   Merry Christmas and welcome to John Lewis, just
            so you know, if you place your order by 8 p.m. on
            December 22nd and the product is still in stock, it
            will get to you by Christmas Day. So we can get
            you to the right person can you tell us, in a few
            words, what your query is about.

ROSIE   You have sent me an incomplete product.

JL   I'm sorry, I didn't quite catch that, please can you
            tell me, in a few words, what your query is about?

ROSIE   The product you have sent to me is incomplete.

JL   I'm sorry, I didn't quite catch that, please can you
            tell me –

ROSIE   You've sent me a bed that doesn't have enough
            legs –

JL   I'm sorry, I didn't quite catch that –

ROSIE   I JUST WANT TO SPEAK TO A HUMAN

JL   I think you are experiencing a few problems; I'm
            going to transfer you to a customer-service
            representative who can assist you with your query.

            Adele plays for a few seconds.

            Hello you're through to Jennifer at John Lewis
            Customer Services, can I take your name please?

ROSIE   Rosie

JL   Hi Rosie
            What seems to be the problem today?

ROSIE   Hi.
            Yeah so you've sent me a bed with only three legs

JL   Okay I'm ever so sorry to hear that Rosie, let me
            see if I can try and sort that out for you, can I just
            take your number in case we get cut off over the
            course of this call.

ROSIE   Isn't it on your screen?

JL   We aren't actually permitted to –

ROSIE   No okay it's fine it's 07654298735.

JL   Thanks for that Rosie.
            That's super.
            Again, I'm very sorry this has happened.
            Can I take the order reference number please?

ROSIE   HL39KY671

JL   Is that haitch for hotel?

ROSIE   It's aitch actually.

JL   Haitch for hotel?

ROSIE   You actually don't say it –
            When you say aitch,
            There's no H.

JL   I'm sorry was it haitch for hotel?

ROSIE   Okay yeah for hotel
            Then L for lettuce

JL   L for lima?

ROSIE   Right yeah sorry I don't know the actual words –

JL   That's quite alright Rosie so we have haitch for
            hotel L for lima 39 K for kilo Y for Yankee 671
            Is that right?

ROSIE   Yeah.

JL   Okay I'm just going to have a little look through
            our system for that, do you mind if we put you on
            hold for a second?

ROSIE   Actually –

            *She doesn't wait for an answer and is put straight
            back onto Adele hold music.*

            ROSIE *is waiting listening to Adele.*

JL   Hi Rosie?
            Are you still there?

ROSIE   Yeah.

JL   Thanks for holding
            So I actually don't appear to have this order on our
            system, are you sure you definitely ordered it from
            John Lewis?

ROSIE   Yeah I am.

JL   Right.
            I hear that.
            It's just that it's not showing up on my system.

ROSIE   Well there's a bed right in front of me that's come
            out of a John Lewis box and it only has three legs
            I don't know what you're trying to say?

JL   I completely hear where you're coming from Rosie,
            All I'm saying is it isn't actually appearing on my
            system.
            But that's okay,
            Just bear with me –
            Just one second Rosie.

            Back to loud Adele hold music.

            Rosie are you still there?

ROSIE   Yeah.

JL   Okay so we've managed to track down your order
            and I can see here that this is actually an external
            product so it's actually not something I'm able to
            help you with over the phone. I'm afraid you're
            going to have to go into a John Lewis store and
            speak to someone in person about this tomorrow.
            Is there anything else I can help you with today
            Rosie?

ROSIE   No, I'm sorry,
            That isn't going to work for me.
            I need the leg before 8 p.m. today, I'm going to
            need help from someone today to sort this out?

JL   Right okay.
            I can see where you're coming from,
            But as I say, I'm very sorry, but this isn't actually
            something I can help you with over the phone,

because it isn't actually a John Lewis own-brand product –

ROSIE   It's called the John Lewis Royal II High-end Bedstead, Super-kingsize?
How is that not one of your products?

JL   I can see how that could be confusing for you Rosie but I'm afraid there really is nothing I can do from this end.
Okay Rosie I can see here that the store on Oxford Street is open until 9 p.m. so if you can get yourself there this evening they might be able to help you out.

ROSIE   Right

JL   Is there anything else I can help you with today Rosie?

ROSIE   No thanks that's it

JL   Okay you have a lovely rest of your day then, take care now, bye.

11.

ROSIE   Things Wren has said to me in the last thirteen minutes:

Rosie are you cross? Because you're walking with cross feet.
Rosie why are you looking like that?
Rosie go away.
Rosie where are you?
Oh Rosie that's a nice dress... Is it a dress or a top?
Rosie I'm a bit confused.
Rosie is this organic? Because the packaging doesn't look organic.
Rosie my ear is itching; does this have tomato in it?
Rosie I'm allergic to tomatoes.
I'll have a Bloody Mary.
Rosie what's wrong with your eyes?

Rosie can we make sure we always wash our hands
before touching me.
Rosie you really mustn't put your phone in that
pocket. You'll get bum cancer.
Rosie, are you depressed? Because you only listen
to depressing music.

12.

We hear the sound of an iPhone ringing.

ROSIE   Sorry
            I've got to take this –

LUCY   Rosie
            Right
            When are you coming back?
            Because there's a disgusting smell
            Yah
            In the office
            I feel like I'm going to vomit.
            It's awful.
            It's so strong I feel like I can taste it.
            So we need to find out what it is asap
            I can't work like this.

ROSIE   Right well I'm at Wren's apartment
            Are Marni or Cressy able to help?

LUCY   Don't be ridiculous.
            They're too busy to be dealing with this –
            They're working in Pret anyway because they can't
            stand breathing it in.
            I can't leave.
            I have some urgent emails to send and a meeting in
            ten minutes –
            So you're going to have to deal with this one Rosie,
            I'm not being unreasonable here.
            Just hurry up with the bed and come back to the
            office as quick as you can
            Yah bye.

As ROSIE *hangs up, her phone rings again.*

WREN   Rosie –
           Are you okay?
           Has something happened?
           Oh –
           I've just been trying to get hold of you for the last
           three hours.
           It's been going straight to answerphone,
           Has your phone broken or something?
           Right well –
           Have you got the bed?
           Because we've decided to bring my babies down
           this evening,
           So we'll need a bigger bed to fit us all in,
           We co-sleep.
           So it will need to be the biggest one you can get
           that fits in the room
           And it'll need barriers, but not plastic ones
           We'll be at the apartment in two hours.
           Also the babies need formula,
           But we want to try them on a non-dairy one,
           So you'll need to go to Whole Foods and see what
           they have.
           I'd like to avoid soya if possible.
           And Rosie we need to make sure there are blackout
           blinds in all the bedrooms.
           In case we decide to co-sleep separately,
           I think that's it.
           Okay see you at six.

ROSIE   Fuck
           Oh for fuck's –

           ROSIE*'s phone is ringing again.*

           Sorry –
           Sorry one minute

           MUM *is on the phone whilst mixing bowl of*
           something.

           As MUM *starts talking, we hear classical string*
           music being played in the background.

MUM   Hi Rose
           Just a quick one,
           I need your advice with something.
           I'm planning the food for when the Talbots come
           to stay
           In July
           Do you think –
           Yes I'm aware it's December but I just need to talk
           to you about the way we're going to do things
           Do you think we should have a roast on the Sunday?
           Something nice like beef or something
           And go on a long walk that day,
           Or do all of that the day before?
           Because they're leaving on the Sunday and it's not
           very nice to travel after a big roast is it?
           But doing it on the Saturday isn't very traditional
           and I don't know how I feel about that.
           Because of course the other option is to just do
           something altogether more modern and non-
           traditional and not have a roast?
           I could just do something from what's-his-name
           Ottellangy or whatever he's called –
           You know the one with all the herbs?
           And then it wouldn't feel odd would it?
           And anyway that's more summery.
           Don't really feel like a roast when it's hot do you?
           Then again you never can rely on the weather in
           July really can you?
           What do you think?

ROSIE   You know what Mum,
           I really don't give a flying fuck what you cook for
           the Talbots,
           I probably won't be there.
           Can't you just deal with this yourself?

MUM   There's no need to take that tone with me young
           lady –
           You've made yourself quite clear,
           I won't bother you any more.

ROSIE   Well I'm sorry but I just have bigger things to be
           worrying about –

MUM   No don't apologise if you don't mean it.
            I'm sure you've got much more important things to
            be worrying about,
            I'll stop wasting your time
            And by the way,
            It was your dad's birthday yesterday.
            Would have been nice if you'd have at least sent
            him a card –

ROSIE   Fuck
            Mum

            We hear the sound of an incoming call on ROSIE*'s
            phone.*

            Timmy is calling and I have to pick up –
            I'm hanging up now –

TIMMY   Hi Rosa
            It's Timmy.
            Are you on your own?
            Great.
            Where's Luc?
            Okay good.
            Look sugar I need you to do me a little favour.
            Yah so the thing is my nest is empty.
            Yah my nest.
            It's empty.
            Yah no the eagle has flown the nest.
            And I need you to fill it.
            Do you see what I'm saying darling?
            I need you to fill it with another eagle or a beak or
            even some eggs but I'd prefer a beak.
            To fill my nest.
            Are you catching my drift?
            Oh come on Rosa!
            Try a bit harder.
            I need some beak.
            I need you to get me some –
            To fill my nest.
            I need you to buy me some cocaine okay.
            Not a lot –
            Just a little dab for me.

And I'd appreciate it if you don't bother Lucy
with this.
She doesn't need to know about this.
Just between you and I okay?
This is what I need you to do,
This will require you to buy some hummus,
I need you to get the charlie,
And Sellotape it to the bottom of the hummus pot
okay?
And then I need you to put it in the fridge right at
the back behind the cornichons okay?
And when you've done that I need you to text me
saying these exact words 'Hello Timmy, I've got
the hummus do you need anything else?'
And then just make sure you're out of the house by
the time I get back okay?
Great.
Thanks sugar.
You're one of the good ones.
Okay bye
Bye bye bye bye bye.

ROSIE*'s phone starts ringing seconds after*
TIMMY *hangs up, she picks up.*

WREN   Hi
            I forgot to say earlier
            This Marni girl,
            Who is she?

ROSIE   She works in the production office,
            She's a part of Lucy's team,
            I think she's an intern,
            Why has she been bothering you?

WREN   She's American.
            She's awful.
            I can't tell what she's saying
            And she talks far too fast.
            I need you to get her to stop.
            I don't want to have to deal with her again,
            Make sure she knows,
            Also I've lost my passport.

And my credit card.
Can you cancel all the Coutts cards?
Okay I've got to go,
My babies need me.

We hear WREN *hang up.*

MARNI *is sitting on her swivel chair again.*

MARNI   Rosa,
What has more carbs in it
An apple
Or a banana?
Because I need to organise my snacking
It's been pretty chaotic recently
And I feel like it's weighing me down
Also, be honest
Do you think I've let my eyebrows go?
I've been trying to let them grow out a bit
And get a bit bushier
Because I'm really into Lily Collins' look
But I think it might be veering towards Cara
Delevingne
And I don't want to look that feral
Rosa?
Pay attention!

ROSIE   Sorry –
I think they look great.
I'm not sure about the carbs.
But look Marni,
Could I have a quick word?
Thanks.
Yeah it's nothing –
I just need to –
Wren has just asked me to,
No you haven't done anything wrong – it's more –
Look.
Could you – ?
Would you mind just –
Not looking at her,
Or talking to her,
Again,

Please.
Don't ask why –
It's not your fault.
Oh god, don't cry!

MARNI *has lost it, she's crying.*

MARNI   What is it?
         Am I too full-on or something?
         Is that it?

ROSIE   Really.
         It's just –
         She'd prefer it if you didn't –
         Talk or look at her.
         Okay?
         Thanks.

MARNI   Am I annoying or something?
         What is it?

ROSIE   Sorry.
         Just come to me next time,
         If you need anything.
         Look,
         Have a tissue.

MARNI   I mean it's who I am
         What can I do?
         My ex always said I was too intense –

ROSIE   Have a tissue and go to the toilets and just cry for a
         minute.
         Just cry.
         And then come back out here and continue the
         great work you're doing with the snacks,
         Just don't look at her okay?
         Thanks.

         ROSIE *is back on the swivel chair with the
         keyboard and two phones, one on either ear, one
         should be the type of phone that would connect to a
         plug socket. The conversations should alternate
         between phones.*

         She is frantically typing.

This sequence could be over music or a beat.

At the end of every phone conversation we hear the dial tone as the other person hangs up.

Hi is that Feather and Black?
Yeah can I speak to someone about getting a
delivery today?
No I know
It's just it said on your website that you were able
to –
Hello?

Hi Bobby!
It's Rosie,
From school?
From Community?
Yeah you know we used to sit next to each other in
biology –
Bobby do you still sell drugs?
Bobby?
Hello?

Hi there
What are the chances of you doing a bed delivery
in the next two hours?
Slim?
Hello
Ikea?

Xanthe
How ARE you?
It's Rosie,
From dancing,
You know we used to do ballet together
Yeah yeah exactly!
I'm sorry about that
I didn't mean it,
I was just insecure.
Girls can be mean at that age,
I'm much nicer now.
Fair enough –

Hi yeah are you still able to deliver today?
Even if we paid you more?

I mean I could pay extra –
I just really need a bed delivery this evening.
No I'm not joking.
Stop laughing.
It's not funny.
That's really fucking rude.

Hi Ralph
How's the anthropology going?
…Sorry Ralph I'm gonna have to just stop you there
I'm just in a bit of a rush –
Well actually, I was wondering, this is really
awkward but –
Are you still into taking stuff
When you're out
Well I don't know, like coke for instance?
Ralph?

ROSIE *is trying to open a bottle of water whilst on
the phone, it's fizzy water and explodes all over her
when she opens it, water covers the phones and*
ROSIE *is electrocuted. We hear a load crack, flash
of white and then into blackout.*

FUCK!
ARGH
FUCK
Oh my god
Fucking
Ow
Ow.

*There is a moment still in blackout when we just
hear* ROSIE *in pain. She doesn't realise what's
happened to her yet and is in a lot of pain and
trying to stand up when her mobile rings.* ROSIE*'s
voice is shaky and weak until the end of the scene.*

The rest of this scene is said in blackout.

Hi
Lucy

LUCY   Where the fuck have you been?
           Did you decide to take a fucking holiday or

something?
Did you think now was a good time to do that
whilst we're all running around with our arses on
fire in the office?
Did you get lost in Whole Foods or something?
I've been wearing a scarf round my face all day.
It smells like something died in here.

ROSIE   No –
God.
Lucy –
Sorry I haven't been in touch,
I've –
I think I've just been –
I just had a really bad shock –

LUCY   Rosie what are you talking about?
I don't have time to hear your –

ROSIE   I was just on the phone,
And the water,
And then
I just
It was such a shock
The apartment is black
I think I've tripped a fuse or –

LUCY   What?
Oh this is a major fuck-up.
How did this happen?
What were you doing?
Rosie I actually can't believe this.
Wren is arriving in half an hour with her children
and she's going to want to make them dinner and
bath them and put them to bed and there's no
fucking electricity?
Be quiet.
Stop crying.
I knew this job was too much for you.
Get on the phone with her agent
Find an emergency electrician
I don't care what you do but you need to sort it out
before she gets there.
Yah bye.

Lights slowly fade up on ROSIE *sat on the floor,*
covered in water and her right arm and hand, up to
her shoulder, is entirely black.

13.

ROSIE   Did you ever have that feeling when you were little,
             When you really liked someone,
             And wanted them to be your friend,
             And you tried so hard to be like them,
             And get them to like you,
             And you pretended to like all the things they liked,
             And laughed at all their jokes,
             And you started talking like them,
             And behaving like them,
             And then by some miracle they sort of let you be
             their friend?
             And you got to spend more time with them,
             And suddenly you're in their circle and sitting with
             them in citizenship,
             And you're all wearing matching glittery eyeliner,
             And you start to hate their other friends,
             And you're jealous of their other friends,
             And every time you see them with someone else
             you wonder what it is about them that they like?
             And you wonder who they're texting all the time,
             And you start wondering what they're thinking
             when they're quiet,
             And whether they hate your perfume because they
             always sort of wrinkle their noses when you come
             near them.
             And you start to wonder if they'd notice if you
             weren't there,
             Or if they'd miss you?
             Because it's always you they forget,
             When they're making plans,
             And it's always you they leave out,
             When they've got too much on their hands.
             And you're trying so hard to get everything right,

And make it look like you don't mind,
But then something happens,
Something bad,
And they look at you,
Like you're the only one who can help them,
And like they really need your help.
And you feel special
Because it's you they've chosen
To sort this mess out,
So you ignore the fact that your arm feels like it's
on fire,
And you try not to think about the buzzing in your
brain,
Or the sick in your throat,
And you try to think in order of priority.
Because maybe if you get everything done in time,
Maybe she'll forget she felt so cross with you a
moment ago
And maybe it will all be okay.
And maybe she'll ask you to come for dinner,
And you can pretend she never called you a cunt
In front of all those people.

Things I've said to myself in the last twenty-nine
minutes:

Rosie have you been in a fight?
Because your arms are shaking and your eyes have
been twitching all night.
Rosie you need to ignore the pain in your neck,
start the day as you mean to go on and try not to
make another mistake.
Rosie the crash wasn't your fault
You looked in your mirror and the other driver
didn't brake
Rosie you've got to tell Ben you can't come to his
birthday and you've got to think of a better reason
than 'Wren needs tickets to Birdie.'
Rosie when are you going to tell Lucy about the
crash?
And are you really all right or does it actually hurt
to get dressed because you've got whiplash?

Rosie try not to think about the way she laughed,
when you ran to get her a drink, fell and hit your
head on the sink.
She was laughing with you and you would have too
if you'd seen the way you flew through the air and
landed in a heap by the chair.
Rosie you need to sleep
Rosie you need to eat
Rosie have you seen your eyes?
They're hollow and dark and it's no surprise.
Rosie it's five thirty-one and you've got fourteen
minutes until you have to be up and about.
Rosie you've been up all night,
So just let your body rest,
Then get up and smile like everything is alright.

We all make sacrifices.
Don't pretend that you haven't,
Some people choose to work,
And others choose to support.
Some people stay married,
And some people get divorced.
And some of us are leaders,
And some of us are not,
But there's no shame in that,
There's no shame in settling with your lot.
There's something to be said for knowing your
limits
And there's a lot to be said for knowing your
strengths.
And maybe hers is in her confidence,
She chose to be a leader
And she chose her husband well,
She knew what she was doing
And he'll follow her to hell.
She might not have any friends,
And she might not be a mother,
But she's a woman in control
And she's a woman like no other.

Sometimes you wonder if she was bullied at
school –

Because you've heard people say that often bullies
are people who have been bullied in the past.
And you think she must have learnt this from
somewhere.
Because one moment it can feel like you are the
most interesting and thrilling person in the room
And like she wouldn't want to be anywhere else
and like every word you say is music to her ears
And the next moment it feels like you're sticking
a rusty nail in the sole of her foot when you look
at her.
Like every word you say is acid on her tongue
And you're making everything she is trying to do
much harder for her.
And you think to yourself that that isn't normal
That you've never seen anyone change themselves
or the way they make you feel so quickly,
That you've never been made to feel this way by
anyone before
And so it can't be her fault.
Someone must have made her this way,
Or maybe it's just you,
Maybe you are the problem,
And you think to yourself,
Maybe you just aren't very good at this,
Maybe you should be trying harder
And doing more
And sleeping less
And thinking more
And fussing less.
Maybe she's right
And it's not that hard
And you need to grow up
And you need to look smart,
Because you might have been electrocuted,
But at the end of the day you're not dead.
Your heart's still beating and your brain's in your
head.
So just pull yourself together and sort this shit out,
Get Timmy some coke and get out of the house.
You've got an hour or so before Wren arrives,

So call every bed shop within a thirty-minute drive.
Maybe there's someone you know who could help?
Grace works near Whole Foods and could sort that
bit out,
She knows what you're dealing with and she'll
understand,
She could get you the formula and that'd be grand,
But then you think about Whole Foods and all you
see is the food,
Because you haven't had anything since that bowl
of soup.
And you feel your tummy rumble,
And you remember the shock,
And the pain in your arm that you thought you'd
forgot,
And there in that moment you realise something,
That for one fucked-up moment you thought that
you should –
Just carry on with your day and shut up and put up
But Rosie, you think,
It's not the end of the world,
If Wren's bed doesn't arrive
And it's not a disaster if Timmy can't get high,
But it would be a shame if you ignored the fact,
That a thousand volts of electricity has just shot
down your back,
And it would be a shame if by the end of the day,
The bed had arrived and the coke was on its way,
But you're on the floor with your face turning grey
And a quiet still space where your beating heart lay.

The End.

CORNERMEN

Oli Forsyth

For N.E.O.N.

Oli Forsyth is a writer, poet, producer and actor from London. He established Smoke & Oakum Theatre in 2013 and staged his first play *Tinderbox* in 2014. *Tinderbox* went on at Theatre503, London, and the Edinburgh Festival Fringe, during this run it was nominated for the Amnesty International Freedom and Speech Award before transferring to London.

In 2015, Oli wrote *Cornermen,* inspired by his experiences in the world of boxing. The show opened at the Old Red Lion Theatre before playing at the Pleasance Courtyard, the New Diorama Theatre, Otherplace Brighton and finally the VAULT Festival. Oli's other works include *Aubade* (2015), and *Happy Dave* (2016), and a self-published collection of poems in 2015.

'Now, whoever has the courage and a strong and collected spirit in his breast, let him come forward, lace on the gloves, and put up his hands.'

Virgil

Acknowledgements

Special thanks to Charlie Butt, Fenella Dawnay, Julia Tyrrell, Lucy Danser, Ed Harris, David Hall, David Byrne and New Diorama Theatre, Mark Burford and The Ring Boxing Club, Stewart Pringle and Old Red Lion Theatre, The Pleasance Theatre Trust, Otherplace Brighton and the VAULT Festival Team.

O.F.

Cornermen premiered at the Old Red Lion, London, on 30 July 2015. It was first performed at VAULT Festival, London, on 2 March 2016, with the following cast:

MICKEY	James Barbour
DREW	Jesse Rutherford
JOEY	Oli Forsyth
SID	Andrew Livingstone

Director	Joe Lichtenstein
Producer	Oli Forsyth
Lighting and Sound Technician	Adam Bellamy
Video Editor and Image Design	David Hall

Characters

MICKEY
DREW
JOEY
SID

Scene One

*All four actors sit, ready, in a line of four stools behind a
canvas on the floor. The canvas is the stage, whenever an actor
takes to the canvas they are 'on stage', when they exit the
canvas they are, in effect, invisible. The lights focuses in a
square of light onto the canvas as* MICKEY *takes centre stage.*

MICKEY. It's cyclical this boxing game, keeps on turning, that's
why it's all rounds and rings. The second one lot are done, the
next generation are starting all over again, heading to the same
place in the same way. It's because we love it. The only reason
we know David beat Goliath is because everyone who
watched kept talking about it. Make two people fight and the
spectators will come. But no one wants to watch an old fighter.
We like young blood. So when you've thrown your best shots
and you don't move as well as you used to, that wheel will
take you right back to where you started, poor with no
prospects, and now twenty years older. So every boxer has a
choice, either they stay on the wheel and hope their time at the
top gets them enough for the journey back down. Or, they can
get off, and use that wheel to take them places.

Transition. MICKEY *returns for his stool as the scene moves
into 'The Pub' where* MICKEY, DREW *and* JOEY *sit
searching for ideas. They have been here for some time.*

JOEY. Mark Francis?

DREW. He quit.

JOEY. What about his brother?

DREW. He quit too.

JOEY. Wasn't there a cousin? Swear those boys had a cousin…
Paddy?

DREW. Peter?

MICKEY. Paul. And he quit at around the same time.

DREW. Besides, none of them were exactly champions, were they?

MICKEY. We're not after champions, are we? We just need someone who can put on a show and sell a few tickets.

JOEY. And stay on his feet.

Beat.

What about Ricky Mayer?

DREW. He's got to be about forty now, we don't want that.

JOEY. Well, at the moment we've got no one so let's not discount him just yet.

DREW. We can do better than a punch-drunk pensioner.

JOEY. Oh, can we? Well, if you've got a young, athletic heavyweight stashed away that wants to sign with us then do point him out, Drew. But until he shows up I say we approach Mayer.

MICKEY. He won't do it. Next fight's his last.

JOEY. How do you know?

MICKEY. I asked him a few months ago. What about Shane Andrews?

DREW. Ah poor bloke.

JOEY. Shane?

DREW. Yep.

JOEY. Why?

DREW. Rick Morris put him to sleep in the second about a year back and he hasn't lasted longer than four rounds since then.

MICKEY. Well, what about Rick Morris?

DREW. He quit.

Collective beat.

JOEY. Christ alive, seven years on the circuit and everyone we knew has quit.

DREW. Or died.

JOEY. Or is shit.

MICKEY. Sam Coulson found God.

JOEY (*shocked*). He didn't.

MICKEY. Yeah. Set up a gym in a prison teaching young guys how to box.

DREW. Can't hold that against him.

MICKEY. Offered me a job couple of years ago… wish I'd taken it right about now.

DREW. Freddie Baker?

JOEY. Quit.

MICKEY. Got knocked out by Poulter last year and packed it in not long after. Good call if you ask me, it was starting to show. How about Saul Burton?

Beat.

DREW. He's not up for it, Mick.

MICKEY. What? He's far too young to pack it in, good fighter too. What's his problem?

DREW. No, he's still boxing it's just… he had some trust issues about us, about the group.

MICKEY. Trust issues?

DREW. Yep.

Beat.

MICKEY. With me?

DREW. Yeah. Well, with all of us really.

JOEY. Oh, terrific.

MICKEY. Why?

DREW. He said there was a suggestion we don't treat our boxers as well as we should.

MICKEY. He really said that? What? Because one fighter gets hurt on our watch suddenly we can't be trusted? I mean, Jesus. We make a couple of bad calls and they turn me into a villain!

JOEY. I know, Mick, it was our names getting smeared as well.

MICKEY. But it's me that prats like Saul Burton want nothing to do with. They don't understand. You have to risk things from time to time in life. I mean this isn't golf, it's boxing for Christ's sake –

DREW. Look, all we need to do is sign someone who wins a few fights and moves up the rankings a bit, then all will be forgotten.

MICKEY. Bloody hope so. Can't work in an industry where no one trusts you.

DREW. Who else? Let's think big.

MICKEY. Hold on, before we carry on with this I could... use a break. Shall we get a drink?

JOEY. Go on then.

MICKEY. Whose round is it?

JOEY. Yours. It's always bloody yours.

MICKEY. All right, all right. (*Beat*.) But let's keep going with this first. We need to find someone.

JOEY. Mike Dennit?

MICKEY. He's thirty-something, Joe. What are we going to do with that?

JOEY. Well, exactly, think about it, he's established. We can book fights using his name and we all get paid. Beats scrabbling around trying to build some kid's reputation.

DREW. And in two years' time we're back at this table in the same situation just with another boxer who everyone saw get knocked about on our watch. We don't want old, we don't want established, we need something new. Something that can grow.

JOEY. Well, help me out, Drew, refresh my memory, how did you get started again?

MICKEY *sniggers*.

DREW. I never got past club level really. I wasn't made for boxing.

JOEY. Shocker.

DREW. Because you were such a star.

JOEY. I went professional.

DREW. For five years. And how many fights did you win?

JOEY. At least I went for it.

DREW. But you ended up in the same place as me.

MICKEY. Which is nowhere.

The confrontation subsides.

DREW. Mick, you did all right when you were younger, how did you get signed?

MICKEY. I got picked up at an amateur night when I was eighteen.

DREW. Well, there we are. Let's get to an amateur night, see what's there.

JOEY. No, no, no. If we go down that road we'll end up with some lanky teenager who still needs toilet training.

DREW. And if we keep going through our phone book we'll end up with some old git who's already got the shakes.

JOEY. Mick?

MICKEY. Well, we're not getting anywhere with people we know.

Let's give it a look.

The scenes quickly transitions to 'The Amateur Night'.
MICKEY, JOEY and DREW sit facing out to the audience as if watching a fight.

Scene Two

A bell sounds to start the fight.

DREW. They've had this place redone.

JOEY. They have indeed.

DREW. Used to be a right mess, remember? I don't recognise anyone here.

MICKEY. Well, it's been a while since we last showed an interest in amateurs.

JOEY. Let's not make a habit of it. Right, says here they've got fifteen three-round fights, means we'll see thirty boxers in total, what are we after?

MICKEY. I say middleweight to light-heavyweight.

DREW. Yeah. I can see that. Around the twelve-stone mark.

MICKEY. Not so big he'll be slow but broad enough to pack a punch.

JOEY. Well, these two are featherweights so ignore them.

DREW. We want a worker too. Like Harry Coles, remember? A proper grafter.

JOEY. Okay good, good. Age?

MICKEY. Younger the better.

DREW. But he needs a chin. No good to us if he gets knocked out all the time.

Three bells.

MICKEY. Case in point.

DREW. Saw that one coming a mile off.

JOEY. We could talk to that bloke.

DREW. Nah look at him. Got to be late twenties, we need a bit of youth.

MICKEY. Exactly. It's a fresh start, Drew, we don't want anyone else's bad habits.

DREW. What are these new guys?

JOEY (*checks programme*). Welterweights.

DREW. Little on the light side.

MICKEY. Let's not be picky, if we see someone good we get after them before any of the other managers here do.

DREW. We'll have to be quick.

JOEY. Train them up, turn pro and start booking some fights.

MICKEY. Nice little earner for the next ten years.

DREW. Fifteen if we're lucky.

MICKEY. God, wouldn't that be nice. A journeyman with a good reputation and regular fights.

JOEY. If we could get two or three on the books we'd be –

They all shoot up. Something impressive has just happened in the ring.

MICKEY. Oh!

DREW. Jesus Christ.

JOEY. Big right hand.

DREW. Where did that come from?

JOEY. And again! And again!

MICKEY. Fuck me he's fast!

JOEY. They're going to stop the fight!

MICKEY *springs into action.*

MICKEY. Who is he?

They all look to JOEY.

JOEY. Uh… right, well, says here it's Ferdinand in the ivory trunks and Sparks in the… the noyer?

MICKEY. What the fuck is noyer?

JOEY. I dunno. Ivory is going to be grey, isn't it? Because an elephant is grey.

Beat. They look at the ring.

MICKEY. No one's wearing grey, you tit! I see white shorts and purple shorts.

DREW. Purple shorts! We want purple, that's what magenta is.

MICKEY. Right and what's his name?

JOEY. Sid Sparks. Go get him!

MICKEY. Where's he gone?

DREW. The changing rooms.

JOEY. Get going, Mick!

MICKEY. Jesus, fuck, how do I look?

DREW. Fine, fine. Have you got a contract?

MICKEY. Bollocks.

JOEY. Jesus Christ.

MICKEY. All right.

JOEY. One thing you had to remember.

MICKEY. All right!

DREW. Look, just get a bloody handshake. Guilt him into hanging on, we can get him a contract on Monday.

MICKEY. Right, any of you got a tenner?

JOEY. Get out!

MICKEY. It's a good-faith payment. I'll tell him there's more to come. No kid turns their back on money.

JOEY. It's not coming out of my pocket.

DREW *quickly hands over ten pounds*.

MICKEY. Okay, right, Joey, come with me, stand outside and say you're the doctor. Make sure no one else comes in.

They break.

Scene Three

The scene resolves itself into 'The Changing Room'.
DREW/DOCTOR *is giving* SID *the once-over, checking eye movement, looking for any cuts.*

DREW/DOCTOR. And look into the light.

> SID *does so.*

Okay, and turn your head left.

> MICKEY *enters behind them.*

Any headaches? Pains in the body?

> SID *shakes his head.*

Well, looks like you avoided any damage.

MICKEY. Next fight's about to start, doctor, they need you
  ringside.

DREW/DOCTOR. Right. Right you are. (*Turns to* SID.)

Congratulations, well fought, Sam.

SID. Sid.

> *Beat.*

DREW/DOCTOR. Yes, of course.

> DREW *exits, leaving* MICKEY *and* SID.

MICKEY. You want a team that knows your name, Sid.

SID. Who are you?

MICKEY. Mickey Donovan. You ever heard of me?

> SID *shakes his head.*

Okay, not to worry. I'm a manager, I run a team of three
  other trainers and we all just saw your fight.

SID. Oh yeah?

MICKEY (*hums ascent*). It was a good fight, good stoppage.
  Pretty lucky but good nonetheless.

SID. Come off it. It was a great shot.

MICKEY. I'm not saying it wasn't a good punch. I'm just saying he walked into it.

SID. Why'd he do that?

MICKEY. That's between him and his team.

SID. I think you're talking bollocks.

MICKEY. Well, you're wrong.

Beat.

Are you still in school, Sid?

SID. I'm twenty-one.

MICKEY. Ah. You looked a lot younger out there.

SID. Where were you sat?

MICKEY. Ringside.

SID. I didn't see you.

Beat.

MICKEY. Do you work, Sid?

SID. Apprenticeship.

MICKEY. In what?

SID. Electrical repairs.

MICKEY. I see. Pay well?

SID. It will when they employ me full time.

MICKEY. And when will that be?

SID. A year at most.

MICKEY. You sound very sure, quite cocky for an apprentice.

SID. I'm good with my hands.

MICKEY. I knew that already, Sid.

Beat.

I've got an idea for you. We were all very impressed with how you boxed out there but you're still a long way off where you need to be if you want to make some money out of this. But we all think that, given the right guidance, you could do very well for yourself, have a back-up in case that illustrious career in repairs doesn't come off. So here's what I'm proposing, come on board with us, we'll get you out of the workshop, train you up and turn you pro.

SID. I need the work.

MICKEY. Once you've turned professional the money comes in.

SID. Only if I win.

MICKEY. Not at all, plenty of journeymen make a good wage.

SID. What so I'll get paid to lose?

MICKEY. No, you'll get paid to fight in front of hundreds of people.

SID. But as filler.

MICKEY (*shrugging*). Lose some of the time, win some of the time.

SID. Lose most of the time.

MICKEY. Or you could spend your life fixing lamps and old ladies' radios. Then you'll be a loser all of the time.

Pause. SID *thinks.*

I'd bet you a fair amount that when that bell went, and the ref lifted up your arm you felt a special little thump right around here, where your ribs meet. (*Points to his solar plexus.*) Like you were the greatest thing that ever lived. I can give you that every day, and I can pay you for it. You've just got to box for me.

Pause.

SID. I need to ask my mum.

MICKEY. Fair enough. And if she says yes?

Beat.

SID. I'll do it.

MICKEY. Good boy. Where are you training?

SID. Riley's Boxing Club.

MICKEY. I know the one. Me and my team will come by on Monday morning to give you a contract and start working. Don't forget, don't be late and don't tell anyone what you're doing until we show up, okay?

SID. Yes.

MICKEY. Good. (*Gives him the ten pounds.*) That's for tonight. Spend some of it on your mum.

Beat.

Shake my hand.

He puts his hand out. SID *takes it,* MICKEY *holds on.*

When boys like you break promises like these it has a way of coming back to haunt them. So don't go running off with any flash gits in suits waving pieces of paper at you, got it?

SID *nods. They shake. The scene very quickly snaps back to 'The Amateur Night' with all three in a line watching the ring.*

DREW. And where's he training?

MICKEY. Riley's in Borough.

DREW. I hate that place.

MICKEY. Well done, Joe. Didn't hear a peep out of anyone else.

JOEY. Wasn't much of a problem in the end.

DREW. Just after you left some kid named Ricky Burns put on an absolute masterclass.

MICKEY. Oh yeah?

DREW. Best I've ever seen. Flattened his bloke in the first round. Doctor was only thirty seconds late but nearly missed the whole thing.

JOEY. Look he's only just coming to now, poor kid.

MICKEY. Well, where's this Burns guy then? We could make it two in a night!

DREW. Doubt that. He's right there with the bigger boys. No wonder he's smiling.

MICKEY. Oh.

DREW. Yep. No one was that interested in our bloke after they'd seen that.

DREW *steps forward. Monologue state.*

Scene Four

DREW. We signed Sid Sparks to make us money. That was the main reason. He was incredibly fast, and the thing with quick fighters is that they don't get hit so much, means they fight more, means they make you more money. But the first time I saw him, I really didn't think that much of him. He was an investment, and one Mickey was very keen to cash in on. He'd been talking with this promoter in Brighton who ran a local club. Anyone who came down and made a fight of it got five hundred pounds no questions asked. Way we saw it, Sid got his professional debut, we all got a hundred pounds and if it went well we could start building Sid's reputation as a journeyman. Journeymen are the backbone of boxing, most people only ever hear about the champions and the contenders, the cream of the crop. But the beating heart of this business are the guys you never heard of who fight any opponent and expect to lose. If a journeyman gets a good reputation he can make a nice living out of losing, build a career. But at that point Sid had no reputation, no history and therefore no say over who he was fighting. Which is a very dangerous thing. So only three weeks after signing him, we all went down to Brighton for Sid Sparks' professional debut.

Scene Five

MICKEY, DREW *and* JOEY *snap into a line looking
diagonally across the ring at an imaginary boxer of epic
proportion.* SID *warms up behind them, out of earshot. The
mood is one of fear and tension.*

JOEY. Jesus Christ.

DREW. Oh bollocks.

MICKEY. I know.

DREW. No way on earth is that man a welterweight.

JOEY. He's massive.

MICKEY. I know.

JOEY. He's gonna kill him.

MICKEY. Shut up, Joe.

JOEY. Well, he is. Look at the fucking size of him!

DREW. He's gotta be six two.

JOEY. Did you know this was who he'd be fighting?

MICKEY. Did I know he'd be fighting the Incredible bloody
Hulk? No, Joe, they failed to mention that.

JOEY. Oh my God.

DREW. This is not good, Mick.

MICKEY. I know.

DREW. I mean this is not a smart move.

JOEY. It's his debut for Christ's sake.

MICKEY. Right, all of you shut up. No more talk about Sid
getting hurt, he doesn't need to hear it.

JOEY. We should pull the fight, Mick, we should let him back
out.

MICKEY. And how do we get paid if he doesn't fight? If he
doesn't go in there we leave with nothing so stop crying and
start getting him ready. No one will expect him to last long
so if he can make a fight of the first few rounds we'll still get
that five hundred. Okay? Bring him in.

MICKEY *and* DREW *turn to collect* SID. JOEY *becomes the* REF, *who walks to the front of the stage to deliver instructions to the boxers. All four actors look up to give the idea of the size of the opponent.*

JOEY/REF (*with great relish*). All right. I want a clean fight. Nothing below the belt, no heads and no elbows. When I say break I want a good break. In the event of a knockdown the aggressor must go to a neutral corner and I will start the count of ten. Obey my commands and protect yourself at all times. Touch gloves and come out fighting.

They go to break.

DREW. How you feeling, kid?

SID *nods. Massaging. He begins to bounce and limber up. Shadow-boxing.*

MICKEY. All right, Sid. Time for you to dance. Stay off him for a while. Lead with the left for the first few and keep moving. We can start poking at him when you've found your range.

SID *nods.*

Come here. (*Grabbing him closer.*) There's no shame in going down a little easy. No one wants to see you get hurt.

MICKEY *inserts the gumshield.* SID *turns back, stands, and begins to focus across the stage at his opponent.*

JOEY. Let's be busy, Sid.

DREW. Stay on your toes, watch him tire.

MICKEY. Pop, pop, pop just like we practised, yeah?

The bell rings. SID *trots out into 'The Ring' offstage, controlled and confident.* (*Note, at no point do we see* SID *actually fighting.*)

They watch. DREW *steps forward.*

DREW. That night Sid threw two hundred and fifty punches landing an incredible hundred and thirty-five. He didn't put a foot wrong all night. And we watched, absolutely dumbfounded as this kid came to life under the lights. Before he'd been some kid with quick hands but now... now he was different. Suddenly we realised there was more to Sid than just a journeyman, we'd been sat on a gold mine and not seen it.

Beat.

After that first fight we stayed in the south of England for about a year, fighting regularly and winning, so by the time we returned to London he was already more successful than any boxer we'd managed before. He was a name, which was great for the fights, but it meant he became part of a world that we knew nothing about. Cameras and contracts to fight guys high up in the rankings. And we didn't know how to handle it. On the one hand we wanted to enjoy the success, the glitz and all that, but on the other we could see it was getting to Sid. To go from nothing to a name in eighteen months threw him, and it threw some of us. Mickey though, he didn't blink, he was constantly at every other boxer around. If they were higher than Sid in the rankings he'd do everything he could to make them fight, so the bouts got harder and harder. After one year in London Sid Sparks was ranked as the twelfth best welterweight in the UK and set to fight Mark Hayward, one of the biggest names of the last generation. And we were just about holding on to him.

Scene Six

The scene changes to 'The Press Conference'. MICKEY, JOEY and SID sit in a line. JOEY and MICKEY are covering all the questions that SID fails to answer and loving the attention.

DREW/REPORTER. Sid! Next week you fight Mark Hayward to solidify your place as a top-ten British boxer, nervous?

Beat. SID doesn't answer.

JOEY. Of course we're not. Sid Sparks is the next generation of British boxing and we're ready to show that.

MICKEY (*painfully pensively*). Yeah, and I think what my colleague is trying to say is that it's all about hard work so we've got no reason to be nervous.

DREW/REPORTER. Is that right, Sid? You're not concerned about the gulf in experience?

Beat.

MICKEY. You see experience, we see age. Thirty-eight is not young.

DREW/REPORTER. So you think you can do it? Beat one of the most decorated boxers in British history?

JOEY. Absolutely.

MICKEY. No question.

DREW/REPORTER. Sid?

Beat.

SID. Yeah, I can.

DREW/REPORTER. Okay. (*Moving on.*) Now obviously the big talking point in British boxing at the moment is the rise of new welterwight wonderboy Ricky Burns who recently claimed the British title in emphatic fashion. Did you see the fight, Sid?

SID. No.

DREW/REPORTER. But you heard about it?

SID *looks around for support, then:*

SID. I heard it was quite a knockout.

JOEY. We're not here to talk about Ricky Burns –

MICKEY. Other fights with other boxers are none of our business.

DREW/REPORTER. But they will be if you win next week. If you beat Hayward you'll have to go on to face the likes of Hooper and Kosky and Burns who are certainly not thirty-eight and who are, at the moment, a class above.

Beat.

SID. I take each fight as it comes, I don't want to speculate on –

MICKEY. Sid Sparks is the best welterweight in Britain. When we're done with Hayward we'll continue to challenge up the rankings. If any other boxer thinks they're good enough to beat him you tell us where to sign.

They break. The scene resolves itself back to 'The Pub'.

Scene Seven

MICKEY. He just sat there!

JOEY. Yeah.

MICKEY. Just sitting – not saying anything.

JOEY. Yeah.

MICKEY. It's an interview for christsakes, he had to say something.

JOEY. You'd have thought.

MICKEY. But no, all this 'I take each fight as it comes.' How about selling some bloody tickets?!

JOEY. I hear you, Mick.

MICKEY *sits*.

MICKEY. I worked months to get this fight and he can't even talk it up.

Pause.

DREW. Howard had a point.

JOEY. Eh?

DREW. He had a point. If Sid beats Hayward we're going to have to think seriously about who he fights up the rankings.

JOEY. Slow down, Drew. They'd eat him alive.

DREW. My thoughts exactly but he disagrees, what was it, Mickey? 'The best welterweight in Britain'?

MICKEY. What's wrong with that?

DREW. Asides from the fact it's not true?

MICKEY. Ah, shut up.

DREW. He's not even close.

MICKEY. I was trying to shift tickets.

JOEY. Never know, might rattle Hayward.

DREW. Don't be silly, Joe.

JOEY. What?

DREW. Mark Hayward is the most experienced boxer in the weight class. He's not going to get rattled by some kid and his team mouthing off on TV.

JOEY. Maybe now he's getting older…?

DREW. No chance. He may be getting on but I watched him fight Lanyard at Wembley last year. Tough as old boots that man.

JOEY. Can't be that confident. I heard he's trying to dodge Ricky Burns.

DREW. Everyone's trying to dodge Ricky Burns.

MICKEY. And what was that about Jeff Beck? Since when has Sid been hanging out with pop stars?

JOEY. No idea. I've noticed the hangovers though.

MICKEY. He was a mess yesterday.

DREW. We don't exactly set a great example, having our meetings in here.

JOEY. What's wrong with The Albion?

DREW. Nothing, nothing. Maybe he's just blowing off steam. He's only twenty-four after all.

MICKEY. He should be focusing on the fight. That's his job. Joey, have a word, will you? Try and settle him down, it's getting silly.

JOEY. Yeah, will do. Shall we head back?

MICKEY. Yeah, course. How's he looking?

JOEY. Good as ever.

MICKEY. Is he planting his front leg on the jabs?

JOEY. He's jabbing like he jabs, Mick, since when was his leg a problem?

DREW. Where's his head?

JOEY. Not like he's ever had an issue with nerves.

MICKEY. Maybe not, but mark my words, second Mark Hayward steps into that ring and starts moving about he'll be shitting himself. C'mon let's go.

They walk downstage to the very bottom then turn, in a line, upstage. MICKEY, JOEY and DREW face towards the audience. They are preparing themselves, doing hair, checking pockets, etc.

Scene Eight

DREW. Joe, might not hurt to pack some extra cottons.

JOEY. Yep.

MICKEY. I've got some already.

JOEY. Can't hurt to be prepared. Don't want him to get cut and then run out of gear.

Slight pause.

MICKEY. Might want to pack some extra Vass as well then.

JOEY. I got it, Mick.

Pause.

MICKEY. How we doing, Sid?

Beat.

Sid?

SID appears. He looks tense, ready to fight.

JOEY. Here he is.

DREW. Feeling okay?

SID *nods and sets himself, he's already begun twitching.*

JOEY *starts working his neck and shoulders* (*note: this is done in the way an owner pets a dog, it's unconscious for both parties*). *Gloves on.*

SID. You're all looking very dapper.

MICKEY. Well, someone's got to take the attention off you.

SID. No chance of that.

JOEY. That's it. Good boy.

Pause. MICKEY *has either procured some pads or goes bare-handed. He holds up his hands and calls out the punch he wants which* SID *responds with. They constantly move and bounce throughout this exchange. Boxing is not a static sport.*

MICKEY. One.

SID *instantly responds with a left jab.*

Good. One.

Punch.

Good. On your toes. Come in, one-one, and then out.

SID *starts to bounce, takes a step in, throws two jabs, and bobs just out of reach.*

Again.

Repeat.

JOEY. Stay off him.

MICKEY. Good. One, two, roll and six.

SID *jabs a left, a right cross,* MICKEY *drags his left hand over,* SID *rolls under to throw a right to the ribs/*MICKEY*'s right hand.*

Again.

Repeat.

And then a one-two.

SID *throws a one-two.*

Good.

There is a momentary pause when MICKEY *is still stood in range and* SID *has just finished throwing. He relaxes a tiny bit before throwing a five-five-three-two with incredible speed and aggression. None of these make contact, it's simply a burning-off of adrenalin.*

JOEY. Attaboy.

More rubbing, massaging from all. They slowly group around SID *so he is facing the audience, hands on him like a group of bodyguards.*

DREW. Ready?

SID *nods. They move forward. Lights out.*

DREW/ANNOUNCER. Ladies and gentlemen, in the red corner weighing in at a hundred and forty-three pounds... Sid Sparks!

Lights out.

They huddle upstage-left as if by a turnbuckle.

JOEY *steps forward.*

JOEY. Mark Hayward had been around for years. He was an immovable part of boxing, like the furniture. We were all terrified of what would happen if Sid got caught or lost concentration for a few seconds. Hayward could have knocked him out with either hand and in big fights like that one it helps to have been around a bit. But we were in the same boat as Sid, we'd never been that far or fought someone that good. We just had to hope the work we did paid off. But we had a plan. We knew Sid wasn't going to knock Hayward out, he was hardly a power-puncher, so that fight was going to be decided on points or it was going to get stopped. The longer the fight went the more chance there was of Hayward catching Sid so we focused everything into getting the fight stopped. We had to give the referee a good enough reason to call it off. Now an old-timer like Hayward, he's got one of those faces. Scar tissue on scar tissue, all around the eyes. This big craggy brow like elephant's skin. That was our ticket. Flesh that's been knocked about over the years is easier to split open. And, as he's a right-handed boxer, he'd have taken most of these shots to his left side. So we sent Sid out for that fight with one very clear instruction.

MICKEY (*back in the corner*). Go get that eye.

Lights up, mid-round, all are shouting advice. These should be somewhat coordinated, not just mindless shouting, have a build, moment of doubt, moment of success.

Careful now. Stay off him, stay off!

JOEY. Right! Right, keep your eyes on the right.

DREW. Dance, Sid, side to side! Christ.

JOEY. Wrap him up for fuck's sake, Sid.

MICKEY (*to* DREW). He can't take many more of those.

DREW. Stay off the fucking ropes, Sid, Jesus!

JOEY. Hook's coming, Sid, hook's coming!

Slightest pause as they watch the punch get thrown. Sudden elation.

Good boy! Cut and move.

MICKEY. Double it up, pop pop.

DREW/ANNOUNCER. Ten seconds!!

JOEY. That's it, Sid, keep at him with those jabs!

DREW. Follow him in! Let's be busy!

JOEY. Now with the right, no fucking daylight!

DREW. Yes!

MICKEY. Jesus! Attaboy!

Bell goes. All swarm forward as SID *appears on the stool. Vaseline goes on, water bottles, No Swells, massage, cold coins to ears, etc., etc. Like a pit stop, incredibly efficient and coordinated. The other two work while* MICKEY *talks to* SID.

SID. He hits like a hammer.

DREW. Breathe it in.

SID. He doesn't bloody stop!

MICKEY. Good boy. Good boy. That's it breathe it in. Deep breaths. Now listen, he's running on fumes at the moment, he's got very little left. Keep making him swing and miss, he won't like it. And his left comes down after throwing it, you see that? Just for a second, a little wobble. Means he's getting tired. So every time he throws a left, you're straight in there with the counter, see how that works for a few rounds.

JOEY. Busy, let's be busy.

MICKEY. And keep at that eye! It's starting to really swell up, you see that?

SID *nods*.

Keep poking away at it. He can't last long, soon enough his hands are going to drop and when they do you go straight in with the right, y'hear? Pop it open like a fucking blister.

DREW. Breathe.

MICKEY. I want his eye cut so large you lose your glove in it.

SID *nods*.

DREW/ANNOUNCER. Ten seconds!

MICKEY. Right, on your feet, show him how fit you are.

DREW. Keep dancing about.

JOEY. And stay away from his big shots. He caught you a few times back there.

MICKEY (*placing his hands on* SID*'s face*). Stick to the plan, this is yours for the taking. Go get that eye.

SID *nods*. *Bell*. SID *moves out, the others stay at the turnbuckle*. JOEY *moves forward*.

JOEY. Thing about cuts is they bleed. Obviously. They become big red markers that a boxer is hurt which everyone can see. Now mouths, noses, ears, they all bleed, hit them enough times and they'll start to show it but eyes... eyes are the worst. They gush blood, they're almost impossible to stem, and it's the cut most likely to get a fight stopped. See, to a referee, a boxer with big swollen eyes that won't stop bleeding can't see what's going on, can't defend himself and therefore shouldn't be allowed to continue. Fight gets stopped. For eight rounds Sid had done nothing but jab at Hayward's left eye and the swelling was growing out of his face like a poppy. We had to just wait, either Sid would get caught, or he'd split Hayward open.

Back to the corner.

MICKEY. Good boy!!

DREW. Double it up.

MICKEY. Oh!

JOEY. Now get out, now get out!

MICKEY. Smooth as you like, look at that!

DREW. Don't get cornered.

JOEY. Watch the feet, the feet!

DREW. God, he moves well.

MICKEY. Keep at him, no breathing room!

JOEY *leaps forward.*

JOEY. For two more rounds this went on. Hayward swinging wildly, Sid slipping out of the way where he could and always, always poking at that left eye. Until eventually Hayward walked straight into a right cross and –

ALL (*as* JOEY *lands the imaginary punch*). Boom.

JOEY. Such a pretty river of red like nothing you've ever seen. Ten rounds of swelling and damage all goes pouring down his chest, onto his shorts and dripping down onto this immaculate white canvas. Perfection. Sid kept hammering away and soon you could see these big red marks where Sid was leading him around the ring. Looked more like bullfighting than boxing. On and on around that ring he went until, in the eleventh round, Sid Sparks established himself as a genuine contender, someone to be reckoned with. We were going to have to fight the bigger boys now, whether Sid was up to it or not.

Bell, all group together.

ALL. Ladies and gentlemen, your winner by way of technical knockout… Siiiiiiid Spaaaaaaarks!

All four actors raise their arms in celebration with SID *in the middle, they savour the moment then slowly transition into:*

Scene Nine

All actors are on stage getting ready, they check their appearance in imaginary mirrors behind which sit the audience. MICKEY, DREW *and* JOEY *are all tense and fussing in the mirrors.* SID *is calm and collected.*

JOEY. How do I look?

DREW. How do I look?

JOEY. You look fine.

DREW. You too.

MICKEY. I'm sweating.

JOEY. So am I.

DREW. Why are we sweating?

JOEY. We're nervous.

MICKEY. It's our party, why are we nervous?

DREW. It's not our party.

JOEY. It's a party for us.

MICKEY. Right, but why am I nervous if the party's for me?

SID. The party's for me.

Beat.

DREW. Eh?

SID. The party's for me. It's to celebrate my victory.

Collective 'ooooh'.

What? I won the fight. I get the party.

MICKEY. And who got you that fight?

JOEY. And who got you ready?

MICKEY. Exactly.

DREW. We're a team, Sid. No one got here on their own.

MICKEY. So whose party is it, Sid?

SID. It's our party.

ALL. Exactly.

Car horn.

JOEY. Taxi's here!

ALL. Bollocks!

The tempo increases.

JOEY. Do I smell all right?

MICKEY. There's a stain on my shirt.

DREW. Don't rub it!

MICKEY. What do I do?

DREW. Just leave it.

JOEY. No one will notice.

DREW. They'll be looking at your face.

SID. They'll be looking at me.

JOEY. Shut up!

SID. There's no stains on my shirt.

MICKEY. Do you want one?

DREW. My hair won't stay down.

JOEY. My hair won't stay up.

MICKEY. Am I balding?!

Beat. All the boys look in the mirror to MICKEY.

DREW. No chance.

JOEY. Course not.

DREW. Just a tight cut.

JOEY. It's all the rage.

SID. We're gonna be late.

ALL. Shit!

JOEY. Ready?

DREW. Ready.

MICKEY. Ready?

SID. Born ready.

They all change places and are at the party. They line up at the bar. 'Let's Dance' by David Bowie builds on the speakers.

MICKEY. This is amazing.

JOEY. Look at that dance floor.

DREW. Look at that bar.

SID. Were all these people at the fight?

MICKEY. Guess so.

SID. Wow.

JOEY. Always looks smaller from under the lights.

DREW. Four pints please.

MICKEY. Go easy, Sid.

SID. It's my night off.

JOEY. Go easy!

SID. You lot are no fun.

DREW. Come on. Let's grip and grin.

ALL. Cheers!

They move. Music grows.

MICKEY. Hi.

JOEY. How you doing?

DREW. All right?

SID. I'm Sid.

JOEY. Enjoy the fight?

DREW. Oh isn't he just?

SID. I wasn't worried. You know from the first punch.

JOEY. Never doubted him.

DREW. Oh he's a great boxer, great kid too.

SID. Bled all over me!

MICKEY. Onwards and upwards now.

JOEY. No, thank you for coming.

DREW. What did you say your name was?

MICKEY. I like your dress.

SID. Come on let's get a drink.

JOEY. I love to dance.

MICKEY. So where are you from then?

DREW. Can I get your number?

SID. Sorry I've got a girlfriend.

ALL. Sid's got a girlfriend?

SID. But how about that drink?

ALL. Go easy!

DREW. Fancy a dance?

JOEY. Try to keep up.

They dance into each other and reform as the four.

MICKEY. This is the best night of my life!

JOEY. My head's spinning.

DREW. Not bad for a small investment, eh?! Have you ever been anywhere like this?!

MICKEY. I could kiss him.

SID. Please don't!

DREW. Aw, he's embarrassed.

JOEY. Pissed too, I reckon.

MICKEY. He's right, Sid. We don't want to be working tonight. This is about us. We deserve it. All those years of working with rubbish fighters.

JOEY. In terrible venues.

DREW. For no money.

MICKEY. Exactly. This is our night, so drink it in.

ALL. Cheers!

MICKEY. Let's dance, boys!

They strut out to the other end of the dance floor and begin to move. The music builds and builds reaching a fever pitch before lights out. Short.

Scene Ten

Lights up on SID *skipping with a hungover* JOEY *watching him. The skipping goes on for some time before:*

JOEY. Question for you, Sid. When did you get a girlfriend?

No answer.

You been keeping little secrets from me?

SID. Go away, Joe.

JOEY. What? I'm just asking, trying to imagine what the life of a top-ten boxer is like.

SID. Well, you should have tried harder when you were younger.

JOEY. Those who can't... So when did Heather creep onto the scene?

SID. I was seeing her before I signed with you lot, now piss off.

JOEY. Is that how you charmed her? Being an unsociable little gobshite?

No answer.

No, I know what it is. I know why she fell for Mr Sid Sparks. It's all that skipping. Tell me I'm wrong. Tell me she didn't go crazy for a bit of skipping.

SID. Shut up, Joe.

JOEY. No no, I think I'm on to something here.

JOEY *rises and goes to stand beside* SID. *He mimics skipping. Testing it out. This is very off-putting.* SID *snaps and stops.*

SID. Fuck off, Joe, I'm working here.

JOEY. Well now, that's no way to talk to your team. Bit sore today, are we? I thought you looked a little worse for wear the other night.

SID. Something to say, Joe?

JOEY. No no, nothing. Just I thought a fit young lad like yourself might handle his hangovers a bit better.

SID. How would you know how I handle my hangovers?

JOEY. Well, this might come as a shock to you, boyo, but I've had to watch you train like this quite a few times.

SID. Spit it out, Joe.

JOEY. You like a drink. That's all I'm saying. No shame in that.

Beat.

Go on.

Stand-off over, SID *resumes skipping.*

Probably something your old man liked as well. Dunno, I've never met him but these things do tend to flow downhill.

Pause.

My old man liked a flutter. Y'know? Not too bad either, he often picked a winner.

Slight pause.

But you know what they say, a little knowledge can be a dangerous thing. Bigger the bet, bigger the loss. But that's the trouble, isn't it? Cos if you like it, and I mean really like it, then the loss never seems as bad as the chance of winning seems good.

Slight pause.

I stay away from bookies. I always figured that if something ate your old man, and he tasted good, chances are you'll probably taste all right as well... y'know what I mean, Sid?

No answer.

You know what I mean.

Pause.

Was your dad a dancer too? Cos I reckon the shapes you were cutting last night must've evolved over generations –

SID *stops skipping.*

SID. Jesus, Joey! Shut up!

JOEY. All right, all right!

SID. I'm just saying /

JOEY. I know, I'm sorry /

SID. I'm just saying, I'm trying to fucking work here and you're going through my family tree.

JOEY. I know, you're right. Sorry. All I'm saying is... the boozing hasn't gone unnoticed, and you might want to think about... I don't know, staying in every now and then.

SID *doesn't respond.*

I reckon that's time, old boy.

SID *drops the rope, moves, bobs. Stretches out.* JOEY *notices him stretching and decides to test his reflexes. Throws a one and a one-one that* SID *dodges.*

SID. Not bad for a hangover.

JOEY *resumes and throws a one-two, one-two – one-two-three* – SID *doges all and catches him in the ribs on the last combo.*

I should train like this more often.

JOEY. Five years ago I'd have had you.

SID. Does that make you feel better?

Enter DREW.

DREW. Sid, masseuse is here.

SID. All right.

JOEY. Lucky boy. What I wouldn't give for a nice rub-down every time I worked up a sweat.

SID. Piss off. They really hurt.

JOEY. My heart bleeds for you.

SID *goes to leave.*

SID. He's been trying to hit me, Drew.

DREW. Tragic. How late were you last night?

SID. Yeah, yeah.

SID *exits.*

DREW. I'm amazed he was in today. State he was in the other night.

JOEY. I've had a word.

DREW. And?

JOEY. And what? He listened. He's twenty-four, likes a drink, there's only so much I can say.

DREW. It's not the drinking itself, it's the way he acts when he's had a few. Right little shit. You might need to try again. Did you see him?

JOEY. Didn't need to, I could smell it on him this morning.

Enter MICKEY.

MICKEY. Good morning, all you pretty things.

JOEY. All right, Mick?

DREW. All right?

MICKEY. I am indeed all right. One might say I'm positively giddy.

JOEY. And why's that?

MICKEY *holds up a brown paper file.*

DREW. What's that then?

MICKEY. I've just come from the offices of KingPin Promotions.

JOEY. Yeah?!

MICKEY. Oh yes.

DREW. And?

MICKEY. In three months' time we fight the number-three welterweight in the country, Gary Hooper.

JOEY. You're joking.

MICKEY. Joey, look deep into my eyes and see that I shit you not.

DREW. How'd you get that?

MICKEY. I've been trying to book us a bout with the bigger boys since Hayward. Hooper was keen.

JOEY. Ducking Burns by any chance?

MICKEY. I would imagine that had something to do with it. But his loss, our gain. We decamp to Manchester in two months' time.

DREW. Manchester?

MICKEY. Yeah.

DREW. Why are we fighting in Manchester?

MICKEY. Hooper's from Manchester. He's the bigger name, he chooses where we fight.

DREW. We'll be fighting in Hooper's backyard.

JOEY. Sid's got fans.

DREW. Sure, but they're not going to travel to Manchester for a non-title fight, are they?

MICKEY. It's more than that, Drew. This fight decides who gets to challenge Burns for the title. Or that's how they're going to sell it.

Beat.

DREW. What?

MICKEY. Chances are Burns will fight the winner –

DREW. You're angling for a fight with Burns?

MICKEY. Yes, Drew, of course I am. Why wouldn't I?

DREW. Burns would kill him.

MICKEY. Maybe. Maybe not.

DREW. It took Sid eleven rounds to beat a granddad.

Beat.

MICKEY. They're paying for our gym, our house, our travel, our wages while we're up there and a cut of the tickets win or lose. For that much I'd have Sid fight anyone.

DREW. And what if Sid's not up to it and takes a beating?

MICKEY (*elated*). We still get paid.

Beat. DREW*'s not convinced.*

What's the point of having a boxer at this level if we don't cash in?

JOEY. Exactly.

MICKEY. Good. I want him on every radio channel and chat show there is.

DREW. Sure we want him out so much?

MICKEY. What d'you mean?

DREW. Well, you know how he is. We don't want to make things a bit more... puritan?

MICKEY. Joey's going to have a word.

JOEY. Already had one.

MICKEY. Problem solved. Get him ready, chaps, we leave in two months. Oh, Sidney?! We need your autograph.

Scene Eleven

They break. The scene resolves itself into 'The Train', two seats facing two seats. MICKEY and DREW are already seated. The scene begins with the sounds of a station and JOEY escorting a delicate SID into the cabin and onto his seat.

DREW. Here he bloody is. I was starting to get worried.

MICKEY. What time d'you call this? Train's about to leave.

JOEY. Some of us had to collect Sleeping Beauty.

They conduct this following exchange in full knowledge that SID is there, like angry parents.

MICKEY. Oh, I see. What hour was it this time, Joe?

JOEY. Him and his lady-love were pushing four o'clock.

DREW. Is that so?

MICKEY. Drew, weren't we rising at a similar hour to pack up some ungrateful sod's gym?

DREW. Yeah, that rings a bell.

MICKEY. And I'm guessing that when this wayward child did return home he was a picture of responsibility and sobriety?

JOEY. I'm sorry to disappoint you but he could barely kick off his shoes.

MICKEY. That, Joey, is heartbreaking. Good night was it, sunshine?

Beat.

SID. Yeah... I met Springsteen.

Beat.

DREW. Bruce Springsteen?

SID (*yawning*). Yeah. We went to one of his gigs with Heather and we got invited backstage so I went along. It was good.

Beat.

DREW. Did he do 'Born in the USA'?

SID. Yeah.

Beat.

JOEY. What about 'Dancing in the Dark'?

DREW. Oh yeah.

Beat.

MICKEY. Well... well, you can kiss goodbye to that sort of thing for the next month, we've got work to do.

JOEY. And you better get down to it. No more pissing around with pop stars.

Slight pause.

DREW. Right, I could use a stretch.

He rises.

Cup of tea, anyone?

JOEY. You're all right.

MICKEY. Give him a hand, Joe.

Beat.

JOEY. All right.

They leave.

Pause.

MICKEY. Springsteen, I ask you.

SID *shrugs.*

You all right?

SID *nods*.

Beat.

You should be chuffed. Hooper was guaranteed to fight Burns before you showed up. You must be making waves.

Beat.

SID. Did you see Hooper's last fight? Against Keller.

MICKEY. Yeah.

SID. He's fast.

MICKEY. That he is.

SID. Reckon he's faster than me?

Beat.

MICKEY. Quite possibly.

SID. Why couldn't I fight down the rankings? Hayward was a tough fight.

MICKEY. You fight up, not down. We want to win titles so we fight the best.

SID. Easy for you to say.

MICKEY. You don't want to win titles?

Beat.

SID. Why do we have to rush? Can't I enjoy this for a bit?

MICKEY. You're not paid to enjoy it. You're paid to win the fights I book you.

SID. And what if I lose?

Beat.

MICKEY. I'm sorry?

Beat.

SID. I don't want to be embarrassed.

MICKEY. No, you just want to waste your time by going out every night.

SID. Here we go.

MICKEY. You have got to sort this out, boy. We're aiming at a title here, this is as big as it gets.

SID. Yeah, yeah.

MICKEY. And this time it's not an old man. You think Hayward was hard just wait until you see Hooper box.

SID. I have seen him.

MICKEY. So why are you pissing around like this? I'm trying to build you a career.

SID. Oh fuck off, Mick.

MICKEY. Excuse me?

SID. You're building me a career? As if you were riding first class before I showed up?

MICKEY. Oh, what are you on about?

SID. You're sorted because of me, Mick. All of you are. And when I'm done my name will be your ticket to get the best guys in the next generation and get rich off them too. After this you're set, next forty years or so you're set. I'm done in ten and then I'm right back where I started. What else am I gonna do? Be a doctor? (*Beat.*) I can count the years I've got left on both hands. So excuse me if I enjoy them while they're here.

MICKEY. You sound like a child.

Beat. SID *leaves.*

They break. DREW *steps forward.*

Scene Twelve

DREW. Looking back now, that fight tastes the worst. An event that big would be the high point of most people's careers but… we just weren't ready. We lost Sid in Manchester. Nothing worked, pleading, shouting we even followed him a few times but we just couldn't convince him that all his pissing around might catch up to him. Trying to explain the idea of losing to a guy who hadn't lost yet was… hard. We didn't seem able to do it. And it just felt odd to me. This was a big stadium fight, the stuff of dreams, and we just let it get the best of us. Of Sid. I mean one day we're working in some damp gym with a leaking ceiling, and the next thing you know we're dropped into a state-of-the-art facility, camera crews outside and Sid's face on twenty-foot posters all over the city. But instead of getting on with the job we just fought amongst ourselves.

We are instantly in 'The Gym'. SID *is doing pads with* JOEY *while the others watch.* SID *has done something wrong.*

MICKEY. No, no, no, no!

SID. What? What fucking now? Eh?

DREW. Same as before, Sid.

SID. What you're starting now as well?

DREW. Well, if you were listening we wouldn't be having this bloody problem, would we?

SID. What?

MICKEY. How many times, Sid? You go in after that left to the body and he's going to clock you time and time again.

SID. Thirteen professional fights, I never once got caught like that. Stellar, Michaels, Hayward, not once, not ever.

MICKEY. But this isn't someone you can dance around. I'm telling you, we've watched the fights, you go in like that against Hooper he's going to take your head off.

JOEY. He's not lying, Sid. He'll put you to sleep every time.

SID *softens a bit.*

SID. But, Joe, if anybody can go in and out without getting caught it's me. You know that.

JOEY. Not against Hooper, Sid. He's lightning fast.

SID. What, faster than me?

Beat.

JOEY. Yeah.

DREW. He's right.

Slight pause.

SID. How can you be this negative? You're all supposed to lift me up.

MICKEY. And you're supposed to show up on time –

SID. Do me a favour, Mick –

MICKEY. On time and ready. You were late again this morning.

SID. Barely.

MICKEY. Half an hour late, and another half-hour to get ready. It's not on.

SID. Well, what's the point of me showing up if all I hear from you lot is that I'm not doing it right and I'm going to get a smack? What's the point?

He makes to leave.

JOEY. Sid mate, come on.

MICKEY. We're not done here, Sid.

SID. We are for today. I'm the one who has to go out there so I'll say when we're done. If that left is going to get me hit then you geniuses put your heads together and find a way for me to get at his body without being knocked out.

SID *storms off.*

MICKEY. What an idiot.

DREW. Yeah.

MICKEY. I mean honestly, what are we doing here messing around with that?

JOEY. He'll get there eventually.

DREW. It'll be too late, Joe, he'll get what we're on about after the first few rounds but by then he won't be able to do anything about it.

MICKEY. Unbelievable. Closest I'll ever get to a title and that prick ruins it.

Beat.

JOEY. So what do we do?

DREW *steps forward.*

DREW. By the time we walked out, Sid was barely talking to us. We were stood in the tunnel, ready to go and Mick asked Sid how he was feeling. Didn't even answer, just walked out into the crowd like he was untouchable. Supreme confidence. But the thing about boxing, is that it keeps you honest. If you don't take it seriously, take your opponents seriously, it'll show. And if you've been out every night and fighting with your team. You'll stand out like a sore thumb.

Cut to the corner. All shout encouragement.

MICKEY. Move your head, Sid!

DREW. Back off.

JOEY. That's it, hold him off.

MICKEY. No, no, no.

JOEY. Not to the bloody ropes, Sid.

DREW. Oh Jesus.

JOEY. Wrap him up for christsakes, wrap him up.

DREW. Good boy.

MICKEY. Now, nice and easy, pick your spots.

JOEY. Oh for fuck's sake!

Big reaction.

DREW. It's the third time he's gone to the body.

MICKEY. He's out of ideas.

JOEY. Thirty seconds left, Sid, just stay off him.

DREW. What is he doing? Get off the bloody ropes.

JOEY. Side to side, Sid!

DREW. Cover up!

MICKEY. Oh Jesus.

JOEY. Watch the right.

Big reaction.

DREW. Shit, he's cut.

MICKEY. Where?

JOEY. Just under the right eye.

MICKEY. Oh no.

JOEY. He's out on his feet.

DREW. Hang on, Sid!

MICKEY. Make sure everything's ready. I want that cut sorted by the next round.

JOEY. Got it.

Bell goes. They surge forwards. SID *slumps into the stool, totally spent.*

MICKEY. Water, Drew.

JOEY. How bad's the cut?

DREW. Not great.

JOEY. How're the ribs?

SID *is puffing so hard he can barely speak.*

DREW. Check his eyes.

MICKEY *clicks around* SID*'s face. He responds but not enough.* MICKEY *claps in his face.*

MICKEY. All right, switch on, Sid.

SID. He's so fast.

DREW. Easy, easy, deep breaths.

JOEY. Think his nose is starting to bleed.

JOEY *is rubbing his ribs or applying cottons to the nose,* DREW *attempts to cool the right eye.*

MICKEY. Sid, you have got to stop going in after his body. He's caught you four times now.

SID. I can't get near him. I can't slow him down.

MICKEY. Well, start picking off his head. He can't move quick if he's dizzy.

SID. He'll have me.

JOEY. And stop going to the bloody ropes. Move about a bit, don't make life easy for him.

MICKEY. Exactly. What happened to dancing about, in and out?

SID. I stand off him he just closes me down.

MICKEY. Stay out of the corners and use your left to keep him away. He can't stay fast forever.

SID. And what if that doesn't work?

JOEY *doubles around the team and becomes the referee.*

JOEY/REF. How's that cut?

MICKEY. Yeah he's fine, ref. No problems here.

JOEY/REF. He needs to start protecting himself.

MICKEY. He's fine.

JOEY/REF. If I don't see a change in the next round I am stopping this fight.

MICKEY (*turning to face him*). Why don't you just keep your eyes on the fight and I'll see to my guy, all right?

JOEY/REF *leaves the stage.*

DREW. What's he banging on about?

MICKEY. Says if he doesn't see a change he's going to stop the fight.

The action stops.

JOEY *returns and moves towards the audience.*

JOEY. There are lots of ways to get ahead in a fight and if
you've been around a bit you'll know most of them. It can be
something as simple as gearing up the crowd, or something a
bit nastier like breaking up the padding in the gloves. This is
the murkier side of boxing. If your fighter is in trouble and
doesn't have any answers you need to find a way to give him
the edge. The way we saw it, we hadn't come all this way to
have our chances ruined by Sid not doing his work. It was up
to us. We had to get him an edge.

Back to action. In amongst the flurry of activity MICKEY *is
thinking.*

DREW/ANNOUNCER. Ten seconds!

MICKEY. Drew?

DREW *looks up.*

What d'you reckon?

Beat.

DREW. Yeah.

MICKEY. I mean, he's going to stop the fight.

DREW. Yeah.

MICKEY. Joey?

Beat.

JOEY *nods.*

Drew, give me the juice.

DREW *ducks into his bag.*

JOEY *comes forward.*

JOEY. Nowadays Monsel's solution is banned. But we used to
use it to stop cuts leaking. Slows down the rate of bleeding,
see. But you had to be very careful when putting it on
because, if it got in the eyes, it was incredibly painful. Now,
if someone says 'juicing the gloves' what they mean is that

you put something on your boxer's gloves that will irritate their opponent's eyes. This could be a type of oil or a salve, or possibly Monsel's solution, if you've got it to hand. Sid was already cut so we were going to use it anyway, Mick just rubbed a little bit on Sid's gloves. All he had to do was land a few punches on Hooper's forehead in the next round and hey presto, Hopper's eyes started streaming. Should've taken about two rounds to wash out. Sid only needed one and a half. No one checked. Why would they? You don't expect it at that level and once Sid started landing good shots it looked like any other knockout. And what were they going to accuse us of? Treating our fighter's cut? It could easily have been a mistake.

Beat.

It wasn't. But it could have been.

Bell rings. Lights. In the dark we hear:

DREW/ANNOUNCER. Ladies and gentlemen! Your winner, coming by way of knockout, Siiiiid Spaaaaarks!

They break and transition into:

Scene Thirteen

We're in 'The Massage Room'. It's been a few days since the fight. DREW is examining SID, trying to work out the toll of such a tough fight. He asks him to move body parts, arms, etc., and works on any stiffness.

DREW. Right arm.

SID *rolls his right shoulder in his socket.*

Stiff?

SID. On the back.

DREW *begins to massage him.*

DREW. Enjoy your weekend off?

SID *nods.*

Good. Good. Nice to see Heather?

SID *nods*.

So what did you do? Left arm.

SID. Don't really know. Sort of just sat in my room.

DREW. Ah, that's not good.

SID. I know.

DREW. Whole point of a weekend off is that you use it to... I
don't know, do something a bit more normal.

SID. Yeah.

DREW. Besides, you just got your first professional knockout.
You're usually ecstatic after a win.

SID. Didn't feel like a win.

DREW. I see.

Beat.

SID. You know that glove thing?

DREW *pauses*.

Didn't Ali do something like that to Liston?

DREW. Other way around but yeah.

SID. You ever done it before?

Beat.

DREW. Not personally, no.

Beat.

SID. And Mick?

DREW. I doubt it. It was pretty extreme, Sid.

SID. But you'd all talked about it?

DREW. You didn't give us much of a choice.

Pause.

SID. So what happens now? Career-wise, where are we going
to now?

DREW. Oh. Well. We've been trying to whip up a bit of a storm while you've been recuperating. Trying to call Burns out and get a title shot for you. Obviously the fight didn't go too well but you finished it like a pro and Burns just wiped the floor with Clarke so –

SID. I listened to it. Sounded brutal.

DREW. It was something to see, but the point is he'll be looking for opposition. After Joey took you back to the hotel we all went out after the cameras and tried to talk it up. Mick said Burns was a coward if he didn't fight you, I thought it was a bit strong but, lo and behold, this morning Mickey gets a call from his management 'regarding a potential fight'.

SID. Really?

DREW. He's over there right now as a matter of fact.

SID. So I'm going to fight Burns?

DREW. Possibly. For a title, Sid.

Pause.

Well, don't look too excited.

Beat.

SID. Joe said most boxers are dodging Burns. Fighting down.

DREW. Well, maybe. Makes it easier for us.

SID. I saw Burns fight the night I beat Hayward.

DREW. After you won? I thought you were with the doctor?

SID. I snuck out.

DREW. Right.

SID. And I watched him, from the tunnel.

Beat.

DREW. Okay.

SID. It was the night he beat Narakov.

DREW. I remember. What are you telling me for?

Beat.

SID. Hooper was dodging Burns, right?

DREW. I don't know.

SID. He was number three in the country, could have fought Burns for the title whenever he wanted. But instead he chooses to fight me, to fight down.

DREW. Well, you insulted him on TV.

SID. What, so he risks a shot at the title to settle a grudge match with me?

DREW. I'm not sure on the intricacies of his plan but –

SID. Drew. He fought me because he knew he couldn't beat Burns. So if Hooper couldn't beat Burns and I couldn't beat –

DREW *clocks what* SID *is getting at and stands in front of him. The tone is no longer one of support or sympathy.* DREW *is angry.*

DREW. Shut up.

Silence.

If you had worked harder, you would have beaten him on your own without us.

SID. Drew –

DREW. If you had worked harder, you would have beaten him on your own without us.

SID. I shouldn't be at this level –

DREW. If you had worked harder, you would have beaten him on your own without us. Say it.

Beat.

SID. If I had worked harder, I could have –

DREW. Don't fuck around with me, Sid! You would have – 'I would have'.

SID. If I had worked harder, I would have beaten him on my own without you.

DREW. That's right. You have got to sort this out – (*Points to his head.*) This is what ruins fighters. This. If you start doubting, and feeling sorry for yourself, then you can fuck off back home right now.

SID. Got it.

DREW *is apoplectic.*

DREW. You are Sid Sparks. And you will take any boxer, and I mean any boxer Mick puts in front of you, I don't care how big, or how tough he is, and you're going to get him in front of you and you're going to hit him, and you're going to hit him, and you're going to hit him, until he is unconscious, on the canvas, with a broken jaw and bleeding from both ears, you understand me?

SID *nods.*

Stand up.

SID *stands.*

When these go – (*Slaps arms.*) and when these go – (*Slaps legs.*) you will have nothing left but the scalps you took and the money you got for cutting them off. How much have you got, Sid?

SID. Some.

DREW. Do you think 'some' is enough? For all the years you've got after? For Heather? For your kids? Do you think that'll pay for the house and the car and the suits and the hospital bills?

SID. No.

DREW. Me neither. So, what are you going to do?

SID. I'm going to work.

DREW. That's right. We're going to work. And then what?

SID. I'm going to win.

Beat.

DREW. Good boy. (*Pulls him in and strokes/ruffles* SID *the way you would a dog who's just had a scare.*) Good boy. Good boy. You know we're always watching out for you.

Enter MICKEY *and* JOEY *who see* DREW *and* SID. *They cross and begin to massage and flick punches at* SID.

JOEY. He's back!

MICKEY. Looking pretty as ever I see. How're you feeling?

SID. Bit stiff.

MICKEY. Well, you earned it. What did you do with your weekend then, Sid? Piss away all your winnings?

SID. No.

DREW. Sat in his room apparently.

Beat.

MICKEY. Well, I'll be. Maybe Hooper managed to knock our message into you. I must remember to thank him.

SID. Fuck off, Mick.

MICKEY. All right.

Pause. MICKEY *smiles at* SID.

How much do you love me, Sidney?

Beat.

SID. What?

MICKEY. Would you say your love for me is a family love?

SID. Sure, Mick.

MICKEY. So in the same way I love you as a son, you would say you love me as a father.

SID. Why not?

MICKEY. Father Christmas perhaps?

Beat.

SID. Well, that depends, Mickey, have you brought me a present?

MICKEY (*with a look of mock surprise*). It's funny you should ask that, Sid. (*Brandishes a brown folder.*) In six months' time you fight Ricky Burns, at Wembley Stadium. For the British welterweight title.

Beat.

SID. How much?

MICKEY. We need to hash out the details. This is just an agreement for the match-up. Still need to agree on the number of rounds, referee, glove weight and that.

SID. But roughly?

MICKEY. A lot.

Beat. SID *looks at* DREW.

You'll need a pen, Sid.

Scene Fourteen

They break. The scene is now 'Backstage' at a talk show. SID is sat down as MICKEY *and* DREW *run through the information. Mirrors surround the room. Over the Tannoy we hear 'Sid Sparks to make-up please, Sid Sparks to make-up.'*

MICKEY. Be polite. Be charming. Be funny and sell the fight. Yes?

SID. Yes.

MICKEY. Good. Off you go.

JOEY. Oh, and tell them to go easy on the make-up, don't want a repeat of last time.

SID. Yeah, yeah.

JOEY. You looked like a satsuma.

SID. Piss off!

SID *exits through the door.*

JOEY. He's a real charmer that one.

Beat. They look around.

I could get used to this.

MICKEY. Well, give it year or two, sign a few more fighters, maybe win a few belts. We could be here permanently.

Beat.

DREW. When are you meeting the Burns team?

MICKEY. Tomorrow. You should come along, could use another head in the negotiations.

JOEY. What's left to arrange?

MICKEY. Sticking points really. Glove types, weight and all that.

JOEY. They'll want to make life difficult.

MICKEY. I know. We just have to hope they go along with it.

DREW. And what if they don't?

MICKEY. Then I'm guessing the gloves get heavier and the fight weight goes up.

DREW. To what?

MICKEY. I don't know.

Beat.

JOEY. So what we're saying is that the chances are Sid goes into this fight against a much heavier opponent with added weight on both hands.

DREW. That's not good enough.

MICKEY. It might have to be.

DREW. He'll get nailed.

MICKEY. Look, if we kick up a fuss about any of these conditions they'll just threaten to pull the fight. Burns has already got the belt, it's not like he needs to fight us.

DREW. Well, if that's how they're going to act we should let them cancel it.

JOEY. What?

DREW. If talks break down over a technicality then neither side loses face, Sid keeps his reputation and we buy ourselves another year before we start thinking about Burns again. That'd be a blessing.

JOEY. You don't think he's going to win?

DREW. Come on, Joe. After watching the Hooper fight do you really think he's going to win? Sid doesn't.

MICKEY. Why are you being so pessimistic? He's undefeated.

DREW. Had a bit of help with that though, didn't he?

JOEY. Jesus, shut up. There's people all over the place.

Beat.

MICKEY. You want me to try and get the fight cancelled?

DREW. Possibly, yeah.

MICKEY. Why?

Beat.

DREW. Because he's going to lose, Mick. As sure as sunrise, he'll finish that bout on the flat of his back. And then it'll be over for him.

JOEY. Always a rematch.

DREW. And change what, Joe? I've watched every bout Burns has had since the night we got Sid and he's better than him. He's just a better boxer. So was Hooper, and we can't pull that trick again.

MICKEY. Come on.

DREW. I'm telling you, Mick, we put Sid up against Burns and he loses, we're not back here next week. We'll have to start all over again.

MICKEY. So we start again.

DREW. Just like that? You're forgetting how we got here, Mick. Starting again means another Hayward, another Hooper, not to mention all the fights before he gets back to that level. Hayward was an old man and he got lucky with Hooper, I don't think we get that lucky again. Sid shouldn't be at this level, he said it himself. If he falls out of the spotlight now he'll have to drag himself back into contention with his fucking fingernails. And even if he does, and he comes back, and he gets another shot at Burns, he'll get beaten. They're just better.

Beat.

If we call it off we could buy ourselves at least another year at the top.

JOEY. And leave Burns alone?

DREW. Yeah. I think so.

MICKEY. Turn down a shot at the title? You're mad.

DREW. Surely it's better than him losing.

JOEY. They've all got to lose eventually.

MICKEY. Exactly. And if it's not against Burns it'll happen two years down the line when he's really falling apart. He'll get humiliated in some knackered town hall in Birmingham rather than at Wembley with fifty thousand people watching.

DREW. Better for him though.

MICKEY. Do you know how big the ticket cut is on a championship fight?

Beat.

DREW. No, Mick. I don't.

MICKEY. It's large.

DREW. You're not the one who has to earn it.

MICKEY. Jesus Christ. I can't believe this. He's a boxer, Drew, a prizefighter. That's his job. Our job is to find the opponents and get him paid.

DREW. But your concern isn't Sid getting paid. It's about you, Mick. It's about your pockets.

MICKEY. Well, I'm sorry if that seems callous to you but I don't intend on living the rest of my life in a rented flat above The Albion.

DREW. Neither do I, but if we handle this wrong that is exactly the life we're going to give Sid. When his legs are gone and his brains are scrambled and we've squeezed every last penny we can get out of him then that's the life we'll be giving him.

JOEY. He's not an idiot, Drew, he knew what he was getting in to when he went pro.

DREW. Come on, Jim. He wouldn't know his arse from his elbow if we weren't around.

Beat.

MICKEY. I think he can win.

JOEY. So do I.

MICKEY. And if not then that's the life he chose. I'm not missing my chance to win a title.

The Tannoy cuts through with: 'Sid Sparks to the stage please, Sid Sparks to the stage'.

JOEY. Come on, that's us. Let's watch him sweat.

Scene Fifteen

They break. We are now watching 'The Talk Show'. Canned applause. DREW/ALEC is introducing SID and JOEY/TYLER, they enter one after the other shaking hands and doing the casual talk before an interview. JOEY/TYLER is a grotesque parody of smooth Hollywood types.

DREW/ALEC. Hello, hello, hello and welcome back to *The Late Show* where tonight we're talking to a very special guest. The man chosen to wrest the title from Ricky Burns' hands, the one, the only, Sid Sparks! And next to him actor Tyler Brantree! Now, Sid. You're ranked fourth in the middleweight division yes?

SID. Number four yes, shortly to be number one.

DREW/ALEC. And still undefeated?

SID. Last I checked.

JOEY/TYLER. Whoa.

SID. Since returning to London I've had fourteen fights, won them all.

DREW/ALEC. Now I think most people would be happy with being number four in that weight class and having a nice undefeated record, but it isn't quite enough for you, is it? So on July 25th you'll be fighting Michael Burns for the British. Welterweight. Title. Is that correct?

JOEY/TYLER. Jesus, man, is that right?

SID. That's absolutely right, yes. July 25th at Wembley Arena I'll be taking the title from Ricky Burns.

JOEY/TYLER. Oh my God.

DREW/ALEC. So you think you've got him?

SID (*laughing slightly*). Well, I mean, I wouldn't have taken the fight if I didn't think I could win it.

DREW/ALEC. Can we go on the record and call that a prediction? You're going to win this fight. Care to pick a round.

JOEY/TYLER *and* DREW/ALEC *laugh at this absurd suggestion.* SID *leans out of his chair to look at* JOEY/TYLER.

SID. Tyler, care to pick a round?

JOEY/TYLER *is amazed.*

JOEY/TYLER. Oh my God! Oh my God!

DREW/ALEC. You've got to be joking! You're going to let them pick the round you're going to win in?

SID. Why not? It'll make things interesting.

JOEY/TYLER. That is super-confident, man.

DREW/ALEC. God, this is amazing. So, Tyler, go on, tell us, which round do you want Sid to finish Burns?

Beat.

JOEY/TYLER. I dunnoooooo man, I just – I dunnooooo. It's a big thing to ask, y'know?

DREW/ALEC. You seem overwhelmed by the pressure here, Tyler.

JOEY/TYLER (*looking up*). I mean I just caaan't get over this guy's spirit. He's just got so much truth in him, y'know? And I feel like... round eight?

DREW/ALEC. Eight?

SID. Eight it is.

JOEY/TYLER. Oh my God.

DREW/ALEC. You heard it here first.

SID. Burns betting be watching so he's knows when to book a taxi for.

JOEY/TYLER. Holy hell, man. Boom! You totally got him.

DREW/ALEC. On that note we're going to head to quick break, don't go anywhere, when we come back Jared's going to sing for us and Sid here is going to give Tyler some boxing lessons for his upcoming film *Jailbird 2: The Man Who Flew the Coop*, don't go away.

They break. JOEY *and* SID *wait for the arrival of* MICKEY *and* DREW *in 'The Gym', perhaps putting on gloves and pads, ready for work.*

Scene Sixteen

JOEY. He didn't.

SID. He did.

JOEY. What, he just came out with it after the show?

SID. The cameras were still running. Band was playing us all out and he just leant over and asked me to do it.

JOEY. Star in his movie?

SID. Not star in it, think he wanted me to play a butler or something.

JOEY. Well, I hope you told him you were busy.

SID. I did.

JOEY. In no uncertain terms.

SID. Absolutely.

Beat.

JOEY. Star in a movie. Honestly.

SID. Act in a movie.

Beat.

JOEY. No one ever asked me to star in a movie.

SID. Well, I'm shocked, Joe, I really am. Hollywood's poorer for it.

JOEY. Ah shut up.

SID. Temper, temper.

MICKEY *and* DREW *enter.*

JOEY. All right? How did it go?

DREW. Not great. Mickey rolled over like a bloody dog.

MICKEY. I did not roll over.

JOEY. Define 'not great'.

SID. I'll go get changed.

DREW. No, no, stay here. You need to hear this. They got everything they wanted.

MICKEY. Drew –

JOEY. Gloves?

Beat.

MICKEY. Twelve ounces.

Beat.

SID. Okay.

JOEY. Fight weight?

MICKEY. Top weight allowed is a hundred and fifty pounds.

Silence.

JOEY. He fights at a hundred and forty-three pounds, Mick.

MICKEY. I do know that, Joe.

JOEY. A hundred and forty-three. Means when he steps up to fight Burns he's going to be seven pounds lighter than him.

SID. And my gloves will weigh four ounces more than usual. Did you get me anything?

MICKEY. Asides from thousands of pounds?

SID. Oh sorry, I didn't realise money is going to stop him tearing me apart. Did we get anything that will help me in the fight?

MICKEY. Fifteen rounds.

Beat.

They wanted twelve rounds, we got fifteen.

JOEY. Oh, well, nothing to worry about then. Storm in a teacup.

MICKEY. Shut up, Joey.

Silence.

It's been two years since Burns had a fight that went past eight rounds. That's two years of early showers and not running the miles. You think he'll be ready for fifteen rounds? No. So you're going to give it to him.

JOEY. Fifteen rounds won't mean a thing if Burns catches him in the fifth round and knocks him out, like he knocks everyone out.

SID. Exactly.

MICKEY. Well, then we don't let him, do we? He wants an eight-round brawl? We don't let him have it.

JOEY. So the plan, as it stands, is don't get hit by him?

MICKEY. Yeah. We work on your feet and your fitness, make it impossible for him to catch you. The full fifteen, that's the plan. Watch him get more pissed off and more puffed up trying to close you down and then bam! Before he's seen it coming we win it on points. We box clever. If he wants your unbeaten record he'll have to wrench it from you.

Scene Seventeen

DREW. And action in five, four, three…

> *They break. Throughout this scene,* SID *cuts between commercials and exercises. They should flow seamlessly into each other. The first commercial is for shampoo.*

SID. Hi, I'm Sid Sparks. In boxing you've always got to keep a clear head. That's why I use Head and Shoulders 2in1 shampoo. The combination of cool mint and soothing Aloe Vera –

DREW. Time!

> SID *is skipping and the team watch, giving him encouragement, this carries on for around ten seconds.*

JOEY. And action in five, four, three…

SID. Hi, I'm Sid Sparks. People often ask me how I stay in such great shape and my answers always the same. Drink British milk. Nothing helps your body like the natural –

DREW. Time!

> MICKEY *and* JOEY *drag a skipping rope across the stage at head height which* SID *bounces under throwing ones and twos as he surfaces.*

MICKEY. And action!

SID. Hi, I'm Sid Sparks.

> *Throughout this exchange* DREW/CHILD *helps* SID *put on his gloves like an enthusiastic assistant.*

DREW/CHILD. Gee, Mr Sparks, you always look so calm in the ring. How do you do that?

SID (*forced laugh*). Well, Timmy, that's simple. I stay calm because I know that if anything happened to me PLO Life Insurance will ensure my loved ones are taken care of. (*Ruffles* DREW's *hair.*) PLO, always keep your guard up.

> *On this final phrase he puts his hands up which, when* JOEY *calls 'Time' stay in place as he does pads with* MICKEY *pushing him backwards, cutting, slipping and landing lots. Throughout,* MICKEY *continues to call out combinations.*

DREW. Good. Time.

They all clap and encourage SID.

Looked good, light, fast.

MICKEY. Ready for some running?

SID *nods*.

JOEY. Course is he, look at him. Ricky who, eh? Ricky fucking who?

MICKEY. That's right, won't lay a paw on you. Come on, more to do.

DREW *steps forward*.

DREW. He'd never looked so good. Totally together, no messing around or going out, he was up every morning to run, work in the day and after training he'd go back to Heather. Perfect. Just like when we signed him.

Beat.

The others seemed to take it all in their stride, maybe they were focusing on the fight, but it really threw me. I couldn't get past the fact that we had signed Sid to be a journeyman, a no one, a boxer who gets paid to lose and be forgotten. And then there I was getting phone calls from new up-and-comers and walking into the dressing room at Wembley arena. And it was all because of him, because of Sid. Guess I should have thanked him.

Scene Eighteen

Back to 'The Dressing Room'. JOEY, MICKEY and DREW are getting ready, packing bags, adjusting jackets.

MICKEY. How we doing, Sid?

Beat.

Sid?

SID *appears.*

JOEY. Here he is.

DREW. Good lad.

MICKEY. Looking good.

They start working on him. Warming up his hands, etc. SID begins to bounce.

Ready?

SID *nods. They face each other. MICKEY throws two elaborate and complex combinations that SID slips, cuts, blocks and evades, finishing each one with a strong counter.*

DREW. Good.

JOEY. Be busy. Good.

SID. Feels good.

MICKEY. Course it does. You're ready, Sid, you're ready for this.

Lots of encouragement, massage, etc. MICKEY pulls SID closer.

When that bell goes at the end of round fifteen, where are you going to be?

SID. On my feet throwing punches.

JOEY. That's right.

MICKEY draws SID closer.

MICKEY. Bring me that title okay?

SID nods.

DREW. Ready?

They all put their hands on SID*'s shoulders for the ring walk as before.*

DREW/ANNOUNCER. Ladies and gentlemen, the challenger, weighing in at a hundred and forty-three pounds, with a record of fourteen wins and no defeats… Sid Sparks!

We snap to the turnbuckle, tense, ready.

Ten seconds!

JOEY. Switch on.

MICKEY. Right. This is it, Sid, time to go to work. What's the plan?

SID. No knockout.

MICKEY. That's right. Slip, slide, move about, if he catches you with anything wrap him up, go straight in with the clinch, get out, set yourself, and go back to jabbing, got it?

SID *nods.*

Don't let me down, okay?

Bell. Out. JOEY *steps forward.*

JOEY. It was very nearly all over in the first round. We should have seen it coming really. These guys had been building up for months, waiting, chomping at the bit, and then suddenly here we are with a massive crowd, and someone says 'go'. Burns came out like a shot, straight at Sid throwing these enormous punches, head, body, hooks, crosses, everything he had. I remember watching him chase Sid around the ring, throwing these knockout shots, you could feel the air coming off them, and Sid's backpeddling away trying to soak them up.

Bell. DREW *steps forward,* JOEY *steps back.*

DREW. We set him straight and got him ready for the next round assuming it would be the same but from the second round on the fight changed. Burns relaxed, backed off, starting really boxing, not brawling. After the intensity of the first round we were all a bit shocked, and so was Sid, he kept waiting for a barrage to come at him but it didn't. Burns just circled around, picked his spots and started jabbing away. No one expected him to fight like that. It was terrifying.

Cut to turnbuckle.

JOEY. That's right one-two. Keep at him.

DREW. Good boy.

JOEY. Stay off him now, go easy.

DREW. Back up, back up!

MICKEY. Why isn't Burns chasing him in?

DREW. He must be banking on a long fight as well.

JOEY. Guess he didn't fancy chasing Sid around if he couldn't knock him out.

MICKEY. Out the corner, out! Out!

JOEY. Good boy.

MICKEY. What so he's just going to go easy all night until he sees an opening?

JOEY. Looks like it.

MICKEY. Well, that fucks our plan right up.

JOEY. What do we do?

DREW/ANNOUNCER. Ten seconds!

MICKEY. If he's changing his plan, we should change ours.

JOEY. To what?

MICKEY. I'm thinking.

DREW. Think quick. Bell's about to go.

JOEY. That's it, Sid. Double them up!

Bell goes. SID *sits, they swarm around him.*

SID. What's he fucking doing?

DREW. Easy, easy.

SID. He's not supposed to fight clever.

MICKEY. We just need to shock him is all, make him revert to his usual way of fighting.

SID. Well, I'm all ears.

MICKEY. Go at him. In this round, go for him. He's not expecting you to come forward, it'll piss him off and he'll start swinging again.

JOEY. Yeah, throw a few more, let go with the punches.

MICKEY. No, don't just throw more. I'm saying the next time you land a jab, Sid, don't back off out of range after. I want you to follow it in with lefts to the body and come upstairs with your right. Scare him, rough him up, he won't like it.

DREW. Up, up, up.

MICKEY. On your feet, Sid. Go get him all right?

DREW *steps forward*.

DREW. It was a bit unorthodox I'll admit, but Mick had a point. Burns and his team had completely sussed us out. All the negotiations about glove size and weight class meant we had put all our focus into making sure the fight went the distance. But when Burns showed up also ready to go the full fifteen we had to try something new or it was home time. We had to rile Burns, upset him, we figured that if Sid could embarrass him, or make him look bad then Burns would revert to fighting in his usual style and we could get on with our game plan. No champion wants to sit back and soak up punches. So at the start of round four we sent Sid out to get him.

Back to the corner.

MICKEY. Come on, Ricky! Make a fight of it!

JOEY. Pick your spots, Sid!

DREW. What are you waiting for? An invite?

JOEY. Don't back off, let him come at you.

MICKEY. Come on, Sid, come on.

DREW. Wait for it, find your mark.

MICKEY. Any second now.

JOEY. Wait for him to come to you.

DREW. Here it comes.

JOEY. We'd been waiting for it all round and then suddenly Burns moved forward and flicked out a jab at Sid's head. He

slipped it perfectly, leaving Burns just off-balance and then…
(*Makes the motion of a left jab as the others sound it out.*)

ALL. Boom!

JOEY. Sid throws out this left.

ALL. Boom!

JOEY. He lands another and then…

ALL. Crack!

JOEY. He lands a right straight onto Burns' nose. More out of
surprise than anything Burns stops moving forward. There
was a split-second pause, and then Sid went at him.

Back to corner.

MICKEY. That's it! That's it!

DREW. No fucking daylight!

JOEY. Keep at him!

DREW. Right! Now with the right!

JOEY. Follow him in!

MICKEY. Stay with him, Sid!

JOEY. Jesus Christ!

DREW *comes forward.*

DREW. The entire atmosphere changed in a second. All the
spectators sat in total shock as they watched the champion,
Ricky Burns, backpedalling away from our Sid, hunched over,
trying to hold back an avalanche. Sid drove him halfway
across the ring with his punches, left, right, head, body, fast as
he could. But you can't throw all that without something
coming back. When Burns hit the ropes he let them take all his
weight, leaning way out and then cannoned back in, slipped
Sid's left and threw the biggest counter he could. It was this
enormous right hook, massive, I saw it starting in his feet and
twist up his body like a spring. A wild, desperate punch but
lethal and right at Sid's head. I watched this huge haymaker,
screaming towards his head, Sid, still surging forwards, Burns
flying off the ropes and then, with inches left, Sid rolled, not
perfectly mind, but he did enough. The weight of Burns'

punch carried on, dragging him around, so by the time Sid came back up Burns was off-balance and unguarded. He was just there, chin up and ready for the picking. Burns watched the punch right onto his chin until...

ALL. Wham.

JOEY. And he went. Like a falling building, there was brief wobble, and then one side collapsed. He dropped to his left knee, his arm draped over the ropes. More like he was catching his breath than anything. The ref rushed in and started counting, Burns was up at four, the bell went, the round finished, and the whole fight changed.

At the corner. A roar greets SID*'s return.*

MICKEY. Good boy!

DREW. Unbelievable.

MICKEY. See how he opened up after that first left? He's been doing it all fight, keep at it.

JOEY. Don't get too confident.

DREW. Yeah, he nearly caught you coming off the ropes.

SID. Didn't though, did he?

DREW. Damn right.

MICKEY. How's that eye looking?

JOEY. Just a bit swollen.

MICKEY. Okay, good lad. Is he looking across at you?

SID *looks over* MICKEY*'s shoulder.*

SID. Yeah.

MICKEY. Good. He's going to come at you now, got it? You embarrassed him and now he's going to try and do the same thing to you.

DREW. Come on, on your feet.

MICKEY. We've got him where we wanted him, all right? Now it's time for you to go to work.

JOEY. Stay off the ropes.

MICKEY. We got a fight on our hands now.

Bell goes, SID *moves into the ring.* JOEY *steps forward.*

JOEY. It's funny watching a fight. See you know your man inside out, from the second he wakes up till when he goes back to sleep you're with him. And then suddenly you're in the fight and you can't do anything. All you get is one minute each round. And you can make little changes, a few suggestions but really you're using that time to stop his nose bleeding and his eyes swelling. You just have to watch as this kid who you've seen grow and change over the years, marches off into the ring, completely alone.

Beat.

He'd had a great start, put down a champion and set the crowd alight, but there's a difference between ready in the gym and seeing it in the ring. When you're fighting someone like Burns they'll always have a little something you didn't expect. And sure enough, by the end of round six Sid was in trouble. Nothing unnerves a boxer like getting hit when he's throwing shots, and Sid was getting beaten to the punch time and again.

SID *flops into the corner.*

MICKEY. Look at the eye, Joe.

DREW. Deep breaths.

MICKEY. Ribs?

DREW. All I can do is ice them.

SID. You said he'd be knackered by the eighth round.

DREW. Well, stop making it so easy for him.

MICKEY. Exactly, if he's not feeling it then make him work more, fucking hit him!

SID. I keep getting nailed with the counter.

JOEY. Side to side.

DREW. He's right. You're a sitting bloody target, keep moving.

JOEY. And get at him.

MICKEY. Clearly he's not slowing down like we thought he would so you have got to slow him down. If you are going to get hit each time you go in then stop messing around with little feelers. If you're going to trade punches with him make sure they're punches worth fucking trading, hit him! Put your glove through his bloody head.

JOEY. Up, up, up.

MICKEY. Stop being so polite, take the dancing shoes off and fucking hit him!

DREW *steps forward*.

DREW. It was the defining round of the fight, Sid was behind on the scorecards and we had to do something to change it. So at the beginning of the tenth we sent Sid out telling him to be much more aggressive, to keep moving forward. Sid wasn't that kind of fighter, but if we let him sit back and soak it up we'd all look bad. We had to make a fight of it.

Back to the corner.

MICKEY. That's it, good boy! Get at him.

JOEY. One, two. One, two.

DREW. Easy, careful.

JOEY. Off the ropes, off the ropes!!

Collective groan.

Get your bloody hands up!

MICKEY. Good lad!

DREW. Now with the right!

JOEY. Attaboy!

DREW. Sid's taking a lot of punches, Mick.

MICKEY. Yeah, but he's giving them too. Go on!

JOEY. Good. Get after that eye!

DREW. He can't keep this up for five more rounds.

MICKEY. It's better than him sitting back and waiting for Burns to take him apart, isn't it? We can't let him have the whole fight his way. You've got to risk stuff, Drew, learn to take risks and hope –

ALL. Oh!

Moment of shock. SID *steps forward.*

SID. I saw them coming. The punches. I saw them. I'd started the round pretty well, taking the fight to Burns just like Mick said. But I'm not a brawler, and I knew I'd slip up eventually. I was pushing Burns back, but I must have thrown one too many because when I saw him winding up to throw the counter I was off-balance. I could see what was coming and knew I had to get out the way but my feet were all wrong and I just had to watch it happen. The jab to my body landed flush just under my heart, stopped me dead. I managed to take some of the sting out of the right cross. But the left uppercut hit me like a train. I felt my legs go and my head snapped back, it's like someone changing the channel, one second I'm watching these shots come in and then suddenly, all I could see were the lights above me.

SID *falls backwards and is caught by the corner.*

JOEY *counts to eight before they hurl him back upright.*

Then he is grabbed and thrown onto the stool.

MICKEY. Water!

JOEY. Is he cut?

DREW. No.

MICKEY. Fucking miracle. You with me, Sid?

Claps about.

DREW. How's your jaw?

SID *has given up.*

SID. I'm done.

DREW. Eh?

MICKEY. He's going to be fine. You've got seven rounds left to steal this, y'hear? Seven more rounds!

SID. I'm done, Mick.

MICKEY. No you're fucking not.

DREW. We could throw in the towel?

JOEY. It was just a bad round, that's all!

MICKEY. He's going to be fine.

SID. I've got nothing left, I'm telling you, Mick, I'm done.

MICKEY. Do you want to quit on your stool? Do you want to be another number on this bastard's record? No! So get back in there and fight. You keep fighting until they ring that final bell!

JOEY. Up, up, up.

MICKEY. Go and get him, Sid!

DREW *steps forward*.

DREW. He didn't even make it through the next round. His legs were shot so he just stood in the middle of the ring and traded punches, bending lower and lower towards the canvas. He got knocked down once more before the ref jumped between them and stopped the fight. The second it was over Burns just turned and headed back to his corner, leaving Sid stumbling around like a pisshead. Job done. It's quite… hard watching someone you care about get treated like that. Outclassed and embarrassed. But he didn't stand a chance, he'd had so much luck getting past all the others that when it finally ran out we saw for the first time how out of his depth he was. Something we should have spotted first.

JOEY *joins* DREW.

JOEY. After the fight we just sat in the changing room. No one spoke, we just sat there, thinking, listening to the stadium empty. When it was all quiet Sid took a shower, and asked Drew to take him home. I figured someone should to talk to the press if we ever wanted a rematch, damage control, so I went out to find reporters. And we left Mickey, sat on his own, just staring at the wall. Zoned out like he'd been the one taking all those punches. So much for bring me that title.

The others drift away, leaving MICKEY *on his own as if in the changing room.*

MICKEY. After that fight I was made. You get someone a title shot, and the world will show up at your front door. The next time I went into work there were five young guys waiting outside my gym, begging me to take them on. No one needed a handshake, no one needed to ask their mum. They'd've sold their teeth to sign with me, which was pretty fortunate as it turned out. One week after the Burns fight I received a letter from the lawyer of a manager named Mark Simmons telling me Mr Sparks has chosen to appoint Mr Simmons as his manager and that my services would no longer be required. That was it, that was all the thanks I got. Turns out Simmons had convinced Sid that it was my fault he lost, my training and my management that let him down, and that if he wanted to win titles he should sign on the dotted line. It was bollocks, Sid lost because he wasn't good enough. At least I got him paid. Simmons got him hurt. But he had a well-known name and a boxer who believed all his promises, easy money. Sid was whisked off as a bit of a novelty, someone for the up-and-comers to cut their teeth on before moving up. He became a journeyman after all, and that title shot never seemed to materialise. He finished with a record of seventy-one fights and forty-three wins. I didn't see him again until just after he retired. I was at York Hall, full house, great atmosphere and one of my boxers had won an earlier fight. They were all celebrating in the changing rooms but I ducked out into the tunnel to see the other bouts. And there he was, standing right next to me, took me a moment to realise who it was he looked so different. Heavier and older, much older than he was, all small eyes and swollen ears decked out in some baggy suit to hide his gut. And he looked like every other boxer you see shuffling around the ring on a fight night, trying to recall their glory days. Because that's the thing about boxers. One day they will come up against someone they can't beat. And it kills them. So we chatted for a bit, I asked what he was going to do now his career was over. I don't think he had a clue. So we just talked about the fights and who was going to win. Then he shuffled off to watch the next generation go at each other. Cyclical, see. We work them, these kids. We grind them and push them and shout at them until one day they can't keep their hands up any more. They start taking punches, and then they don't make any more money. So either they disappear, or they return the favour and go into my line of work. It's not pretty, but we've all got to make a living.

Lights fade to black.

End.

RUN

Stephen Laughton

Stephen Laughton has worked with Headlong Theatre as part of their Headstart writers' programme. In January 2015, his play, *Nine*, was part of the PlayWROUGHT#3 Festival at the Arcola Theatre. Stephen has been involved with various theatres in the UK – he is an alumnus of the Royal Court's Invitational Writers' Group, the Skylines programme at Hampstead Theatre, and he was part of a series of development workshops with the Young Vic Theatre and SoundBites. His first play, *Marina Abramovic is Staring at Me*, opened Terra Firma Theatre's 2011–12 Boxcar Reading Series at the Railroad Playhouse in Newburgh, New York, before moving on to the Cell Theatre in Manhattan.

His work for television includes *Forward* (Blacklisted Films) and *Black Hill* (Lime Pictures). For film, he is working on a script for emerging director Ryan Andrew's second feature film, *The Lake*. Stephen's short drama for young audiences, *Merry New Year*, was broadcast as part of a collaboration between Hampstead and the Roundhouse Theatres.

Prior to life as a writer, Stephen worked as an Associate Producer on a range of critically acclaimed film and television productions, including the Academy Award-shortlisted *Unknown White Male* and multi-award-winning *Tottenham Ayatollah*. He co-directed a short-film, *Recompense*, which screened at the BFI and was an official selection for the New York Independent Film Festival, where it won Best Actor, Best Actress and Best Directorial Debut in the Short Film Category.

'Remember the Sabbath day, keep it holy'

Exodus, 20

Acknowledgements

For Oli, Lauren and Tom – working on this with you is the best.
Ryan Forde Iosco and James Huntrods deserve a big THANK
YOU for hooking us up in the first place, and also for the
original Courting Drama platform and for all your support along
the way. Matt and Sarah Liisa at Nick Hern Books for being
cool about deadlines and typos. Tim and the VAULT Festival
team for letting us in. My fellow Playdaters – Dave Ralf, Isley
Lynn, Chris Adams, Poppy Corbett, Vinay Patel and Sarah
Kosar for love, notes, empathy and understanding. My lovely
agent Nick, and Laura and everyone at The Agency. Just
because. Sue Teddern for keeping me off social media when I'm
trying to skive. Sam, Lee, Rach, Dave the girl, Amy, Gary and
Jack for putting up with my stress tantrums, cat sitting, radar
drop-offs and general love. And Paul, and only partly for
keeping me on top of my Hebrew. I love you.

S.L.

Run was first performed at VAULT Festival, London, on 10 February 2016, with the following cast:

YONNI	Tom Ross-Williams

Director	Oli Rose
Lighting Designer	Peter Harrison
Producer	Lauren Brown
Composer	Helen Sartory
Press and Publicity	Paul Bloomfield

Character

YONNI, *seventeen*

It's chaos in the kitchen.

Yelling. Clatter… shit boiling over

Washing
Spinning…

A dog barking. We don't even have a dog.
So I don't even know what's going on there.

Like it's brown.
About yea big. Yappy.
Keeps looking at me.

I'm worried it's hungry.

But it's mainly jumping around my little brother Jesse, who's grinning like a moron and mirroring the stupid thing.

And it's the happiest I've seen him in months.
Which I guess is good.

And Devorah, my mother, pipes up from her prep every now and then.
Kinda absently telling them to shut up.

And the whole thing is mainly weird.
Kind of adorable.
Somewhat confusing.

I lean down, rub the dog's head, kind of warily.
Pop my bag on the chair.

Devorah proffers a *hi love*, absently asks about the day

There's something too kind in her smile…

And the dog stares back.
With that look…
Head to one side… cocked…
It looks cute but basically means *I wanna eat ya*

And I've never seen it before. The dog.
We're not allowed pets cos of my allergies apparently, and I

can't imagine a world where Devorah would even allow it in her kitchen. I'm not sure it's kosher enough.

But it's adding to this sense of chaos and because tensions already feel high today, and I've got this slow creeping anxiety tightening across my chest, and I just kinda want to go to bed really… I'm mainly too scared to ask why it's here…

Jesse's having fun though. Which from an IQ standpoint makes sense. And it's nice the way my little spaz bro seriously just found himself a soulmate. He's making some kind of Scooby Dooby 'yes he is' kind of noise at it. And basically looks special.

It's Friday.

It's February

It's 4 p.m.

And amongst the scrum, the weekly pre-shabbat panic is officially in full swing. Devorah is frantically cracking individual eggs into a small clear glass. She holds it up to the light. Quickly inspects. Scans to the right, spins to the left. She lowers the glass to see it from above and then lifts it back up to check below.

Satisfied with her inspection she tips the egg into her left hand. And oozes the yolk back to her right.
Then left.
To her right.
And back…

The white of the egg drip-dripping into the bowl below.

She cracks and repeats.

Cracks.
And repeats.

Orders me to chop carrots and I begrudgingly begin.
Soon working out that Jesse's in shit again.

Devorah's berating him over this week's misdemeanours – including the dog… Knew it. And something about detention… again… and his general backchatting attitude shit.

And there's barking and jumping and chopping and cracking
and Jesse's vaguely jigging about the place. And answering
back. Thinking it's all a bit funny.

And it builds and it builds and it builds and it –
Stop.

Breathe.

I fucking hate carrots.
Seriously like proper repulsed by them
And she knows it.

They look gross. Orange actually offends me. And you
cannot… *seriously* cannot… boil a carrot without it festering
everything it touches with its limpity carroty bollocks.
They ruin.
Everything.

And as I hack at the carrots she chimes up –
No one needs to eat your irritation my darling…
That sweet sweet smile again.

Well don't make me chop the fucking carrots then.
I don't say that.
Obvs.

Just tut, and…

Breathe.

And on my in-breath Devorah lets out an exasperated *oy* as she
empties another eggy glass into the waste-disposal-unit thing…

Blood spot.
On the yolk.

She grabs a fresh glass. Stacking up the tainted, sullied glasses
next to the sink.

And as she places it, the dog knocks into her and she lets rip at
Jesse. She won't tell him again. *Get that thing out of the kitchen.*

And then back to beating the shit out of the egg whites.

Reuben, my father, walks in. He drops a bottle of Kiddush wine
onto the counter.

And takes in the scene.
Grunts.

Leaves. He's fun like that.

But Devorah doesn't notice.
I don't think she notices him at all any more.
It's like they somehow just exist in spite of each other these days.

In periphery.

I can't remember when I last saw them talk.

Whites now mixed and I can't help but pick up the rhythm...
and I can feel it in my chest as she slaps in the matzo and starts
forming the dumplings.
I put the knife down.

I need to just –

Breathe.

It's chaos.

It's about one forty-five.

Another Friday, maybe a year ago probably a year and a half
ago now and lunch is nearly done.
Teachers sweep the perimeter, and we're all in huddles...

It's muck-up day today...
And the Year 11s, me and mine, get to bolt after next period...

Study leave.

Or as we like to call it getting stoned with your mates all week
then fully cramming with the geeky kids you've hung shit on for
the last four years the night before your Modular Science exam.

Then passing.

And there's buzzing and manoeuvring and rowdiness in the air.

The kids in my year all excited 'bout egg and flour and maybe
the odd firework. Some kid trying to convince us to catapult
chickens at the school walls.

I hope they're kosher.

And in the rabble I spot you.

Smiling, a bit too cool, somewhat removed…

Still soaking it up…

Like, the day after we met, like properly… At that bus stop…

And you're standing there…

Like. Grinning…
Like that.

Hot.

Blue-green eyes.
Messy hair. Cute smile.

You're fair.
Not like me.
Intellectual. Less like me.
A nice Ashkenazi boy.

You're deep. Literal… Something of the artist…
Bit more like me…

Wry.
Watching it all unfold.

Then you spot me.
Nod.

And I freeze.

Eyes locked.

One…
Two…

And I brave it.

Walk over.
Leave my mates behind as they head off to get whatever
supplies they think they need for whatever little juvenile ploy
they'll play…

Then it's us. Alone.

Hey. You say.

And it's fully disarming.
Kinda calming.

But before we even get to say another thing I look up and there she is.

Devorah.

Raging.

In the middle of the playground.
Dragging Jesse behind her… that kid is always in shit.

And I freeze and she's instantly all over me…

As the rabble returns…

And she's all like… *we're going*… and I'm like *no*. No way. *It's my last day of…* But she's having none of it. She's not coming back and I'm telling her I can make my own way home and everyone's watching and she's like, *don't answer back Yonni*… and everyone's watching and she tells me we're leaving and before I can argue and everyone's watching, I'm warned that I better not start as well.

And everyone's watching.

Everyone.

And I'm horrified.

And we lock eyes, you and I, and you mouth to me… you ask me if I'm alright.

And the whole thing seems to swim…

And everyone's watching.

And in the –

Shame.
That rises.
The the panic… that rises…

You hold me.
With your gaze.

And as as as I'm led away…

Head down… whispering frantically to Devorah about how embarrassing she is, not really paying attention to her total eppy about her meeting with the Head and Jesse and his Hebrew teacher Mr Weiner and how Reuben is probably gonna go batshit crazy –

You catch up.

Pull me back for a second and I'm torn between you and Devorah and I glance back at her and as I do you pull out a pen…

Start to write on my arm… I guess it's muck-up day, so it's kinda what you do yeah…?

But she's calling me back and I pull away.

Smile. Apologetically.

Clock what you've written.

And exhale. Realise I've been holding my breath.

Adam.
07590 –

And I commit it to –

Stop.

And blur.

Later.

As Reuben rages. Jesse is sullen.
Devorah looks between… her perception, her focus, her interest conflicted.

Afflicted.

She appeals to Reuben's sense of reason.
But that's long gone and the word suspended rattles around the room.

SUSPENDED.

With such force that it threatens to bring down the foundations.

Suspended…

Which is kinda what it does to the room.

Suspended.

And I sit and I stare, like not entirely sure why I have to be here but soon find myself completely embodied within this entirely fucked-up scene... And looking back I find myself almost agreeing with Reuben's fervent polemic... that maybe it was the mood of the summer itself taking a stranglehold on our family and that maybe it created the catalyst to the long slow implosion of our absolute entirety... maybe those rising tensions over war in Gaza and all the shit in this city, all the Sieg Heil salutes and the security at school and the swastikas on street signs and the name-calling on Facebook and Twitter and the windows smashed at that synagogue in Belfast and that rabbi attacked in Gateshead and the mutilation of that Israeli lady in Colindale did indeed make it just super fucking shit to be a Jew in pretty much any British city last summer and maybe that fear and and and and that frustration found itself directed.

Projected.
Infected.
Home.
And maybe that's what caused my little brother to go batshit crazy at Mr Weiner cos he was really living up to his name that day...

And maybe that's what's sending my ridiculous little yampy fuck of a father, with his totally embodied small-dog syndrome bullshit even more crazy today and fuelling this total overreaction...

And maybe that's why Devorah finally explodes.

And fuck does she...

And it builds and intensifies and Jesse sobs and Devorah cries and Reuben thunders.

And then she slaps him.

And I'm completely stunned. Shocked into silence.

Because *Reuben* slaps her back.

And she doesn't retaliate. No.
The ear-splitting silence is enough.

She takes Jesse's hand. And crosses the room.

Reuben's mumbled apology lost in the gulf.

She reaches the door and barks my name.

Yonni… she says.

Like it's an order.

Yonni.

And we all just stand there…

I'm Devorah's boy all over.
Except I'm a better cook.
Kinda have to be.

Like I'm really particular about my roast potatoes. And as I go back into the kitchen I clock Devorah basting like a maniac – I say basting… she's shovelling litres of…
I mean.
She's essentially deep-frying them, right.
But in the oven.
And I have to find a way to save them because I'm not sure my stomach can handle all that schmaltz today.

I don't think I can really handle much. Today. If I'm honest.

I ask if she's going Carmelli's. To pick up the challah.
She counters that I could go to Carmelli's.
I offer that if she's getting beigels too, she might need the car.
She questions the amount of beigels I think we need.
I point out that we all like beigels very much.
She requests that I quite literally get on my bike and go fetch challah and beigels.
She also suggest I might want to stop being a smart-arse.
I remind her that she has another son, with a dog now, who might need a walk…

She stares.
Head to one side… cocked…

Go to Carmelli's Yonni.
Don't make me ask you again.

'Kay. Alright. Okay.

And that's my potatoes fucked.

I walk round to the garage and I jump on my bike.

I've still got your stickers all over the seat, the ones from Jew camp.

And I'm cycling down the Queens Road and I think about how excited I was when I found out you were going.

Like, I nearly couldn't be arsed. I've been doing LJY-Netzer shit since I was like... I dunno, like ten...

And I didn't even know you were into the whole youth-movement thing... let alone thinking about Hadracha. As if you could ever lead anything... And I start making lists and spreadsheets of the shit I need to buy and

Stop.

First. Day. Blur.

And whether it's the luck of the draw or a little behind-the-scenes fudging it turns out I'm in your dorm.

And your bunk is next to mine.

Well that's mainly because I've chosen the one at the back. Far end.

And all the arriving plus the intro stuff multiplied by the dinner divided by the benching to the power of the songs equal a really long fucker of a day.

I crawl in to bed.
Exhausted.

Pull the blanket up and notice I'm reciting the angel prayer in my head.

Beshaym Adonai Elohay Yisra'el
Mimini Micha'el
Umismali Gavri'el
Umil'fanei Uri'el
Umayacharei Refa'el
Ve'al roshi Shechinat El.

I dunno why...

Just enjoy…
How…
How lovely it is…

How safe it always makes me feel.

GCSEs are over.
Summer's here…
And I dunno.

Cos I've got the wall to my right.
And you to my left.
My own Michael. My own Gabriel.
And maybe, for now I don't even need Uriel or Raphael.
Maybe I feel actually safe.
Actually.
Happy.
Protected.

And safe.

I've turned slowly onto my left side and I face you.

You're even more beautiful in sleep.

The room glows an eerie green from the fire escape and and as I synchronise my breath to yours and on your in-breath I breathe in and on your out-breath I breathe out

I will you to turn over.

To smile at me.

But soon fall into deep dead sleep and lost somewhere in the twilight of my thoughts, I dream of blue, and time itself hustles and hastens in the gloom and in no time at all I blur into waking and you're there.

Smiling.

Stop.

I've overslept, and you didn't want to wake me, so you stood.

Waiting.
And I smile back at you.

Stop.
Wish I could take a picture.

But you tell me to get up… there's loads to do today… ▪
And I look at you. At you. At beautiful beautiful you.

And I jump out of bed and I catch the smirk in the sideways glance, the way your eyes pass quickly over me.

And that look gets me through the blur of the day.

And…

Later.

Everyone has gone to bed… I'm reading about the fall of the Austro-Hungarian Empire and you tap me on the shoulder… tell me to shut the fuck up before I've even said a word and you gesture out.
And I follow…

To the garden.
In silence.

Pass the tennis courts.

The weird knobbly tree thing.

The toady-pondy-bridge thing.

And I'm soon transfixed.
On your fingers, no less, as you slowly roll the joint.

I'm fascinated. No. Spellbound.
Like enchanted by… by –

The delicacy.
Dexterity.
The intricacy of the movement.

And before I know it you've sparked up and you pass on and I draw in –

And the THC hits me as you land on Venus.

Because if you were an alien, or or or or from any other planet you'd be from Venus…

That feels right, it goes with your eyes.

And I ask why, ask *what's so cool about Venus* and you tell me how it rotates anticlockwise.

And how the atmospheric pressure of Venus is ninety-two times greater than Earth's.

Geek.

And that makes sense to you... in your head... cos that's sometimes how it feels sometimes...

Like overwhelming I guess and the way you make yourself so vulnerable to me.

By telling me that –

– and the way your brow furrows and your stubble bristles and your eyes tear a bit make me fully realise that –

Stop.

You explain how Venus is the hottest planet in the solar system which totally makes sense cos you're like seriously smoking...

And it's the second brightest object in the night sky.

Of course it is.
You're luminous.

Then you ask what planet I'm from?

And I'm nowhere near as articulate or philosophical or actually as geeky as you are.

So you suggest that I'm from Ganymede.

There's water on Ganymede.
Deep, deep down below the surface.
And you reckon it's warm.
And you tell me how Ganymede radiates Aurora, and that it has oxygen, like there's not enough for us to breathe, but it's oxygen nonetheless...

And that's pretty fucken cool, no?

And your whole shtick just... makes me –

Stop.

We're back in the dorm. A mess of clothes and books and shower gel and just boy stuff seems to entangle and sprawl on the bunks below.

I'm wired. Paranoid. Kinda cold.

We've smoked pot at the end of the tennis court again.
Crept back into the house
Tiptoed through the room.
It's haunted you said.
I grin as I'm brushing my teeth.
And you're telling me about some fucked-up murdering vicar
dude.
That's what you get, I pipe up, *when you base a religious system
on original sin.*
And you nod.
Very good, you say.

And you brush past me as you walk into the toilet.

It's gentle. Accidental.
Fully kinda mental.

And we both clock it.

And quick as a flash you're back.
Brushing your teeth too.
Grinning again as you blatantly steal my toothpaste.
You've never used the whitening one before.
Your mum always buys the sensitive stuff.
Less abrasive apparently.

And I steal these glances
In the mirror…

…and I don't know where to put them.
What they mean.

We spit at the same time.

Our hands brush and suddenly you take it…

I think you do. Maybe I do. I don't know cos the world has
stopped and your look asks me if it's okay

And it is oh my god it's okay it's like so okay so just please just
do it just like please just do it just please.

And time itself feels like it's been affected by the weight of this.

And lips almost touch
And I inhale you.

And my heart stops.
And my world stops.
And my

     everything

          just stops.

And we kiss.

       …backwards turns world the and

        fuck
        I
        don't
        even
        know
        which
        way

And
Everything.

     Deep in me.

Just…

Stop.

Austria. You creep into my bunk… Wake me up with a kiss. I
whisper. Tell you I'm exhausted. *I can see*. You say.
And you pull me close.

Are you gonna sleep here…?
But you can't… and it makes you sad. It makes me sad.
You can do anything you want. And as I say it, I think I really
believe it.
It's so hot up here you say
And I'm proud of my reply. I been studying my science…
Well… Wikipedia.
That's because heat rises.
And you play the brief pause for all the drama you can.
Well why is space so cold then? Eh? Tell me that brains…?
And you're so proud of yourself, I kinda don't want to tell you
that.

And we spoon and we chat and we fall asleep.

Until we're rudely awakened.

And my pleas and my panic are lost in the accusation, all lost in
the punishment as we're kicked off camp and you're given
some kind of warning.

I always order in Hebrew at Carmelli's.

I've been doing it since I was like six.

The woman in there, Mrs Carmelli, has pretty much watched
me grow up and week on week we run through our little *how
are you* exchange. She's too busy and can't wait for Shabbat, I
either love or hate school…
And can't wait for Shabbat.

Sh'tayim challot v'tesha beigelim bevakashah

She busies about sorting it.

I work out that I'm probably not gonna eat much tonight so I
should fill up now.

I'm tempted by cream cheese and lox.

I check out the pastries.

Gam ahat bourekah.
Tah-poo-ahkh ahdahmah.

We banter more.

There's this look she gives me, that seems to penetrate my
everything as she asks me in English if today has been okay.

I nod. Quickly. Look down. Quickly.

And pay. Quickly.

Leave on a *todah* and cycle back down Golders Green Road.

Fall deeper into your orbit.

Venus pulling Ganymede, closer to the warming sun.

It's freezing in the bedroom.

I'm close, close, closer still
And feel your warmth as we cuddle up
You're wearing shorts?
It's freezing.
It's summer.
Your house is really cold.
I think you're just scared.
I affirm that yes I could potentially be freaking the fuck out.
And you assure me that it's okay.
We're just gonna kiss and cuddle and nothing's gonna happen.
Then you grin.
Unless you want it to.
And although I do… nothing happens.

Because we want it to be right.

We want it to be conscious.
Well that's what you said and although I don't quite get it, I
think I agree.

I certainly don't wanna be *unconscious*. Right?

And we kiss and we slowly fall asleep, feet and arms entwined.

And I wake in the night with a start, and gently uncurl myself
from you and I head out into the labyrinth in urgent search of
the loo.

And I'm super-tired and can't be arsed to lift the lid so piss into
the sink, absently make a note that I probably need to drink
more water… at least lay off the coffee and and and suddenly
like fucking fuckety fuck like fully horror of horrors as a
precariously balanced toothbrush tumbles right into the jet
stream and FUCK.

So gross.

I wash it.

Twice.

With soap.

Twice.

And I come back to the room and you've moved in the bed and you're naked, and although I knew you were naked, I felt you were naked, I just didn't expect to see you actually naked and I crawl into you and it's still so cold and we sleepily kiss until you wake and it suddenly suddenly feels right and we're tangled and knotted and fully submerged...

And as we tumble through space in this new co-orbital configuration an axis somewhere shifts and it kick-starts a series of aftershocks that fundamentally change everything.

Devorah's burnt the chicken.

Knob.

And she's literally flapping around like a psychopath as the pre-Shabbat panic turns into full-on freaking the fuck out.

I'm like trying to be the calming influence, yeah, like fully fucken zen, suggesting that maybe she just takes the skin off and wrap some pastry round it. She asks me if I'm mental and I'm like *Jamie Oliver does it*.

What about the bones?

I tell her it's fine. *If Jamie's not concerned about the bones I'm not sure we need to be*

I really don't understand why she's fussing so much and you can tell I've hit a nerve but she's being patient with me.

I kinda hate it when they're being patient with me.

She's wittering about salmons in the fridge and that she might do them instead and we can have the chicken for lunch tomorrow after shul and I tell her no one actually gives a shit really and she tells me off for my language and I instantly get over-defensive and she clocks it and she takes my hand, and apologises and tells me it's okay. She understands today is hard and she can do the rest and *do I want to go relax?*

Hot spray hits me and I gasp.

Step closer into the stream. Close my eyes as I wash my hair. I
don't want to scrub too hard. I don't want to wash you away.
I'm good at this now. I've turned washing, but just skin deep
into an art...
And I think about the first time you clocked me in the shower.

As I turned round you were standing there. Watching me...

Saying I look fit.
That you've got something to show me...

Oh yeah, I say...

On the iPad.
A whale has been washed up on Dungeness Beach and there are
rescue teams trying to get it back into the sea.

It's been there all night and it could die and you wanna do
something we should do something.

And you tell me how they can explode.

That in the process of decomposition, methane and other gases
accumulate in the body and and the build-up of pressure, plus
the disintegration of the whale's flesh, potentially causes the
whole thing to burst.

It's cute when you get excited about telling me stuff.
You ask me what I think.

I hope they can save it.

You explain, slowly, cos I'm a dumbass that your parents are
back tomorrow and that you want one last adventure before life
starts again and I have to go back to Devorah, and going to
Dungeness to check this out could be perfect...

Yeah. It could.

Sea blurs sky blur as the wash blurs the wind and this isolated
milieu against this desolate headland that's dominated by these
two massive power stations is bare and bleak and wild and
windswept and just so so so hauntingly beautiful.

We walk slowly down the long long boardwalk.
In silence.

Wrapped up in the empty eeriness all around us.

Dungeness is Britain's only desert and the beach shelves sharply and the currents seem sure and strong.

I'm mesmerised as we walk across pebbles and shingle and watch the waves crash onto the beach. The coast is rugged and the sky feels vacant.

Flotsam washes up and around whilst ubiquitous junk and jetsam seem to whisper their own memories and history.

And as I lose myself you suddenly take my hand, and start singing Leonard Cohen at me, spinning me up and around and about…
First dance at our wedding you declare…
Really? You've thought that far ahead?
You shrug. Say maybe it's me that's been thinking that far ahead and now I'm just projecting it onto you.
Yeah. Okay. But you're the one who's really into Cohen.
You agree. Yeah you are. And you carry on singing at me.

In the voice.

He sings a few lines of 'Dance Me to the End of Love' by Leonard Cohen.

And you spin me under your arms as you whisper the sweet beginnings of our own memories before you twist me out and pull me back and then face to face, kiss me, and send me spinning off –

And then we spot it.

And then we stop.

She's small, around twenty-two feet.
You reckon she's probably a young humpback.

You start telling me that adults are like forty-eight to sixty-three feet in length, that they're known for their magical songs, which totally relay over like huge distances to mainly attract mates but also to just communicate…

And that noise pollution in the sea is really problematic for them and one of the main causes for beaching… and you tell me how the only day on record when whales' stress hormones noticeably

decreased was in 2001, the day after 9/11 – the day when noise
and ship traffic also decreased. Because across the world...
Hundreds upon thousands of ships were confined to port.

And on that day, for the first time, in –
I don't even know how long...
The whales could finally hear one another.
And they could talk to one another.
Sing and shout and call to one another.

On that beautiful day, they reconnected to one another.

Most of the crowds and the news crews have dispersed.
There's a couple of dog-walkers and some kids running about.

But it's mid-afternoon now and the novelty factor is waning
along with the hope and people have shit to do like make dinner
and do their washing and live their inconsequential little lives
and I can't take my eyes off the dying magnificent beast.
You ask someone what's happening.
The quick response is nothing.
The slightly longer one is that we have to wait for the water to
rise.

And you check for the next high tide... and it's like five hours
away.
And the whale is dying.

And it looks hopeless, and it doesn't feel right to leave her to the
crabs and the wind, and it feels like we have to stay with her.

So we do.

And we spend ages on the beach trying to find some kind of
container and when we do, we spend the next few hours
pouring water all over her.

Just the three of us.
Me. And you. And Sophie the Humpback Whale.

That we met on Dungeness Beach. And we tell her we're really
chuffed that she's hanging out with us and we promise her that
we'll do our best to get her home.

And a few hours later, when the three of us have fully and
intimately shared our war stories and the tide seems to be rising
a little as we proper move into the total friendship zone and it's

clear she'd really rather stay... more dog-walkers inform us that she's too high up on the beach for the water to reach her and there's no one to really come and help...
And I don't know what to do.

Panic rises and...

I sit next to Sophie, she's lying on her left side and her right eye is open, staring skyward. Her lower jaw is open too and I notice the long baleen filtering plates.

And they're beautiful and as I look into her eye, an eye that's as big as my fist, I see my own reflection.
And in that deep dark orb I also see fear.
Real fear.

And I can't keep it in and I almost yell that we have to do something.
And we do do something.
We knock on doors.
We get a spade.
We dig a channel so the water can get to her.

Because she can't die, she's just a baby, we can't let her die.

And within about forty-five minutes we have maybe ten, maybe like maybe twelve people and we've dug a small trench and we start to heave...
And it takes us a further thirty minutes to get anywhere.
But we do.
We get there.

We start to move the whale.

And... and it's hard and feels hopeless and panic continues to rise and I can see that panic in Sophie's eye, the one eye I can see, I see the panic there too and I hope she can understand, I hope she gets that we're trying to help her but there's also a sense of calm in her so maybe she does. Maybe she gets it.

And as a group we push and we roll and we thrust her back out into the sea.

We make it.

And I linger with her, trying to get her deeper, deeper... deeper still.

And I'm not a great swimmer and the current is strong and I get her to a depth where she can move... a depth that's maybe out of my depth and and as as as exhausted as she is... as weak as she is...

She manages it.
She swims.

And before she goes, before we lose our connection for ever, I take one last look at her and she looks back at me and I'm positive that I see gratitude.

And then she's gone.
For ever.

It's rowdy round the table.

Lights. Candles. Family. Shouts.

Reuben... mixes grape juice with the wine for Kiddush.
He pours it out...

Takes the cup in his right hand, passes it to his left, and lowers it back onto the palm of his open, outstretched right hand.
Holds it there...
Still
Steady.
Approximately, no, exactly nine inches above the table throughout

Unmoving.

Baruch atah, Adonai he says
Eloheinu melech haolam he says
borei p'ri hagafen he says

Amein we say
L'chaim we say

And then he brandishes the challah...

Baruch atah, Adonai he says
Eloheinu, melech haolam he says
Hamotzilechem min ha'aretz he says
I whisper it under my breath... It's like the easiest blessing and it's just gone...

Like gone.
We eat.

And I struggle.

Food's gross. Conversation's hard.
And these people are harder.

Granny repeats. Uncle and Reuben bicker.

And I feel drowsy, drowsier… like I haven't slept in days. I
haven't slept in a year really…
And the slow creep digestive sleep claws its way up from the
inside out.

And I lose myself.

And everyone around the table.

And I stare at you.
Just.
Stare.

And when I finally pull my gaze away it's already the after-
dinner blessings…

Reuben chants to the rhythm and Devorah, my uncle, Granny
and Jesse keep pace.
But I lag.

I just want today to end.
Devorah offers drinks. And it feels like Reuben's still not happy
about my poor show.

I was the best at Hebrew on Kaytiz.
I even gave you lessons.
I mean you're pretty good yourself but my mum's an Israeli
so…

Uncle asks me about college. He always interrupts. I nod.
Smile.
My parents discuss a party down the street, pre-bar mitzvah, we
should go.

I excuse myself. Say I'm tired. Can I go to bed now please?
Another warning look from Reuben. I should help with the
dishes.
But Devorah tells me it's fine. I look tired…

I'm wired, bent double like an old beggar… Hunched under the double duvet that serves to block the twisted nematic light-modulated crystals that glow from my iPad. Because Devorah thinks turning the wifi off is some kind of no-tech-on-Shabbat deterrent because Devorah doesn't quite understand the concept of 4G or a data package.

And as I hide away in my little man-made blanket booth, I pretend like it's Tishrei… like I'm in my own tiny Sukkah, like I get to tune in to my own tiny world in my own tiny space like a radio tuning all around me.

Click to click to click to click as tabs and panels jump up and about.

And I tab Fetty Wap. All quietly. Click. Who rose to prominence with his 2014 single 'Trap Queen', which was a sleeper hit that peaked at number two on the US Billboard Hot 100 chart. Click. And I like that song. A lot.

He sings a couple of lines of 'Trap Queen' by Fetty Wap.

And I tab Twitter *click* where we don't agree with who's been kicked off #CelebrityBigBrother. And I tab Facebook *click* where Vin is being stalked by an unstoppable robotic assassin on his birthday and Mike's watching cats and Sam's got the best mum in the world and Kanye's bigger than rock and Lee wants one ov these I dunno what it is and we still can't find the llama's and Fetty Wap's vocals are vibrating through my mattress and my hips are rocking out to his rhythm…

He sings a few more lines from 'Trap Queen'.

And I think about what you're doing right now…

And now. And now.

And that every time I'm doing something… that so are you… that there's whole life… outside of me – life… this whole place where you've been present. Where I'm not.

And I want to be there…
Watching what you'd do.
Listening to what you'd say…

And I want you to touch me.
I miss your touch.

And your face feels so far away… and I need help… to get to you.

So I quickly, click, search for images… to help… to get me – – to you…

Hot Jewish guys. Click.

The IDF guy holds a prayer book, wears a dirty vest and tefillin.

But I click away because it…

Doesn't.

Stop.

And I click back on Twitter and we're posting photos of dogs protecting penguins and click through to #richkidsofinstagram and tap tap tap on the door. Me down. Screen down. Silence. Down. Shush.

Devorah's asking if I'm okay.

I'm fine I say.

Are you sure? she says.
I don't want to tell her how much I –
You'd tell me?

MUM.

Because we're here if you –

Stop.

They're going out she says.

Will I be okay? she asks
I will. I think I'll be alright.
Soon.

Night love, she says.

And off she goes.
And I count.

From ten.
And soon… before nine… I imagine you.

Like I do.

In the dark.

Blue-green eyes.
Messy hair. Cute smile.

Us two aliens. At either side of the solar system… Venusian you.
Ganymedian me. This little ET. Trying to call you home.

And I google you because you're always here… Close…

And the picture… and the headline
NO
…and the number… fifth that year.

No.

Third at that particular –

NO.

…I click away.

Onto your Facebook.
No.

I don't want to see what's on your Facebook.

I imagine you in tefillin… click.

Wrapped… all around your arms…
Holding you.

Taking you. Being taken…
And I get into you. Think about you. Get really into…

You message.

The vibration from my iPad rousing and I read and I tap back
straight away…
Weird… I was thinking about you…
Ping. *Be weirder if you weren't no?* Smiley.
Dunno… Smiley.
Ping. *Why wouldn't we be in some kind of communicative synch
that transcends all of space and time?*

You're so fucking clever I love you.

Ping. *You didn't come today.*

I'm sorry.

Ping. *You okay?*
Ping. *What you doing?*
Shabbat. You?

And I wait ages for your reply…

My heart beats in my mouth. Fast. Fast. Faster still. Waiting.
Where you gone?
Waiting. Again.
Fuck, have I upset you? I read the messages back.

Twice.
Trying to find something I missed.

Twice.

Ping. *Shabbat. Sorry. Visitors…*
Ours has been quiet.
Ping. *Everyone's been here today. I swear they're still with the*
Rabbi. Fucking Frummers…
You can't say that shit
Ping. *Just did.*
Ping. *Come Gants Hill*
I wish you could come to Hendon…
Ping. *They're right here…*
So how can I come to Gants Hill?
Ping. *They're leaving soon… some bar mitzvah thing*
Yeah and mine.
Ping. *Come then.*
It's ages
Ping. *It's like half an hour*
It's like the other side of London
Ping. *Cab?*
Money?
Ping. *Tube then.*
Ping. *Come on.*
K. K.

And I can't wait to see you.

My heart is racing as I sneak out.

They would kill me for this. Especially Reuben. He takes
Shabbat way too seriously and –

Northern Line blur.

Bank. Blur.

Change.
Blur.

This is a Central Line train to Hainault via Newberry Park. The next station is Stratford. Please mind the gap between the train and the –

…lad on the other side of the carriage is kinda hot. He's older. Maybe thirties… I've clocked him checking me out a couple of times now. I think about fucking him. It's gone almost as quickly as I think about it.
He smiles though. Nice.

Good arms.

I turn round to open the window thing. The mix of sweat, booze and curry is making me reel.

I pull out my phone. Nothing new on Facebook. Or Twitter.

So I open Grindr.

I never open Grindr. It's just something me and my mates do when we're fucking around… A hundred profiles flash up all around me. I check mine.
The pic is cute. It says I'm cut. It says I'm versatile. It says I'm nineteen. Only some of this is true.

Then come the pings.
Badboi Online
Forty feet away
(insert chest pic)
(insert ass pic)
(insert cock pic)
wanna fuk?
Ur cute

It's him. I flash a smile.

Ready. Aim…

You into younger?

Yeah. He says.
How young?

Young young. He says. He asks for pics. I tell him to go first.

Ping. Ping. Ping.

He's got a pretty decent dick on him and it goes on like that… my teasing, him sleazing across the carriage. He knows it's me. Asks to see my ass.

The picture's not mine but he doesn't know that. It's convincing enough.

I ask for his… Get him to make all the moves… Get him to keep it coming. Keep up like this until I get off.

Then I close the app.

Think about you.

Delete the app

I message you.

Under the park clock. Ten minutes…

I wait.
And I wait.

Ping. *Five.*

I'm smiling. I can hear my heart thump-thumping across my chest and echoing around my body.

I reach into the inside pocket of my jacket and notice my mini-Zohar is gone. Annoying. My kippah is there though. The oversized knitted one Aunt Ada made for me. It's so ugly and big and obvious and white and urgh and I put it on ready to do my impression of Dungeon Master Rabbi Bloome cos that always makes you –

I swear he's a midget
Like officially?
Like he's no way over five foot.
And you called me a knob. And it was the most beautiful moment of my life. Cos you looked at me with such –

Dungeon Master's the educational lead on Jew camp and he's not anywhere as clever as he thinks and the fucker got us booted off and he's round with a funny walk and I pop the kippah in place and I start practising the walk and I'm immediately, firstly, kinda primarily aware of the matched pace.

Then in peripheral I count three.

I pull myself upright. Knee-jerk as much as anything…

There's something about the intensity. The pace.

I speed up.

So do they.

I turn towards the park.

So do they.

And I'm suddenly really scared for a laundry list of reasons, I'm afraid of them because well basic maths and and and I am entirely aware, like fully engaged with all the ways that they could hurt me, and I know that regardless of how hard I could fight back, bottom line – they're a group, they're a three
A triad
A troika

A a a a triumvirate

A triptych

A fucking trinity and that makes me laugh a bit but doesn't really hide the fact that words may well form and clash and jump around my head but they don't quite silence that underlying rumble… three equals the upper hand and if they start I'm fucked.

I cross onto Valentines Park.

So do they.

Two behind. One to the side

I have one hand in my pocket fumbling around for something that I could use to defend myself because these numbers do not pan out for me. The key goes between the first and second fingers of my clenched fist.

And then I remember the kippah.
I pull out my phone. Message. Let me know it's not just me…

I'm nearly here.

Click Facebook

I'm wearing the fucking kippah.

Click. Olive has made a giraffe, Buzlie links to a bunch of randoms who've crushed it and I forgot to wish Vin a Happy Birth–

What you looking at?

Stop.

One on each side.
The other in front.

A triangle.

Slow, Dough and Ho.

I dunno why I call them that... Partly I guess to undermine them... Partly to steady the rising anxiety tightening across my chest... Partly cos Slow looks special, Dough's a bit fat and Ho's wearing too much make-up.

I feel like I'm standing tall but I slightly buckle

Just off to see a friend.
I stammer it out...

Ho says she likes my little hat.

It's not that little actually.
Don't say that.

I do say thanks. And I move my hand up to take it away, start to walk on, but Dough has snatched it...

Panic rises.

And he's put it on wrong – like at the front... cock... *that's not how you wear it you fat fuck*... and he is doing like this really shit German accent... asking Ho and Slow if the Yid-Lid suits him...
Fury rises. They laugh. I shake.

My hands are back on the keys...
My entire body tenses...

I want to go ape-shit
But I quietly ask for it back please

Shame rises.

Dough chucks to Slow and I try to swipe
Dough pushes me back
Slow catches... Shame rises.

Slow puts it on.

Something about looking like a dirty little Jew bitch
And I try to take it but he chucks it to Ho.

And I take a step forward but Dough pushes me back...

And she chucks it back to Slow.

And he stands there sneering at me.

And my shame rises panic rises and my vision swims...

He pulls out his lighter.
And he tries to set it on fire...

My whole everything immediately reels and I think I hear the
word Heeb... and something about an oven and and and

And the red that I see. The entrancing, vivid, all-encompassing,
devastating, overwhelming, humbling profoundly vivid red
that's completely overtaken my line of vision, that's flooded my
brain and my throat and chest and my arms and my fists and my
fists explodes all around me and before he can react I am all
over him.

My first punch breaks Slow's nose.
My second takes him out.

And my rage and my fury and all my my ferocity just detonate
and I try to stay calm and I try to imagine you but I swing round
as Dough punches me in the back of the head and –

Click.

Nothing as I hit the ground and Ho kicks into me

I try to imagine...

Click.

Tefillin

And I grab Dough's foot and pull

Click

Nothing as I manage to roll out of Ho's way and Dough tumbles

Click.

And I pull myself up and the real rage, the you rage in me
builds and I want to fucking kill him.
And with each kick… as I remind him what a little fucking
bitch he is

I think of you…

How you'd never let these morons anywhere near me.

I think of you…
How you'd leap to my defence if you were here…

You.
Umismali Gavri'el …

You.
Of the the the last time I saw you…

Skinny grey jeans.
Woolly grey hat.

We're both heading home for Shabbat, both sad that we can't
light candles together.

Yet. You say.

And I dunno what happens, I don't remember how but we go
from zero to ninety in about two seconds flat as I spark up some
lame-arse comment about *Sex and the City*, and how vacuous
defining yourself by shoes is and before you know it we're
screaming in the street.

Screaming.

And you're trying to make a point but I'm talking over you.
I'm a bit of a fucker like that.
And you try again.
I block.

And again.
Block.
Can I go on, you demand…
Is it a useful comment? I counter
Well I don't know because you won't let me make it.
Well think about it before you do, because if it's just going to
fuel this –
You not letting me speak is completely fueling this…
No, I think you'll find that's your overreaction.

And on and round and up and down…

And you're about to jump in and I stop you again. Warn you
off. Again.

And then it erupts.
You do.
Suddenly.

And you tell me, yell me in my face to shut the fuck up.

SHUT.
THE.
FUCK.
UP.

And I lose it.

Oh my god, do I…

And in the accusations and assertions and the shouting and the
shoving
And the shouting
And the shoving
It all gets fucked
And brittle
And messy
And it builds and it intensifies and I can't remember what I've
said but it basically amounts to fuck you, really to fuck you…

And you're upset, because we've never fought like this before.
I've never had a go at you before.

But it's because I'm upset too.
And I can't handle being this upset.
Not with you.

And I still don't quite know how we got from just super-excited to spend time together to you just just just raging off on your bike.

You're not gonna be my punchbag you yell back.
No one fucking speaks to you like that…
And you circle back.

Demanding to know who the fuck I think I am?

And that look in your eyes as you shake your head.

And that sudden and complete disconnect as you ride off…

Just –

I call and call and I call and I call.

And I message and I Facebook and I call and I call.

And and and shame rises.
As you ignore me.

Over and over and over again.

And I panic. When your phone shuts off.

And.

Panic.

When I get the call two hours later.

Panic.
Rises. And the shame the shame the shame just just
Just just just just just

STOP.

Row after row after row of searing white fluorescent strips beat down and rinse out the sickly pinks and greens of the hospital waiting room whilst bleached disinfectal pungency mask vomit and god knows what else.

It's supposed to be a vaguely decent hospital this one but I guess all A&E departments orbit at least one of the nine circles of hell.

Devorah paces back and forth and the constant a-clacking is like scratched nails across a chalkboard.

Jesse tells her to sit down.
She does.
Tells us she's worried.
Wants you to be okay.
She's sure you are.
Yeah.

I say.

Yeah.

Half-convinced.

Head goes into hands as I lean forward and try to hide into my lap. Try to scrunch myself up into the smallest possible me and tuck myself away.
And I push.
Further.

Smaller.
Smaller.
Smaller still but before I even get the chance to go on, the door swings open and I just know it's going to be good.

And I stretch out and as my eyes adjust to the light as I take in those same eyes and those thin lips and that kink in the hair of of of of of –

– of this person of this woman that isn't you and I notice her empty smile and her empty eyes and try to listen to words I barely grasp because my head swims and my eyes fill and my stomach churns as your mum, as as as as Gabby, chokes out the words.

The word. Singular.

Gone…

Gone where?

Gone.
I want to vomit…

Gone.
I need to leave.

She tries to make it better by touching my arm, tries to hold me.
I'm trying to open my mouth but I can't say anything any more
because I've lost the – the
the
the
capacity
to talk
and with a now well-oiled fight-or-flight response kinda
permanently triggered I pull away
from this some kind of gentle embrace and I think I leave…

I think I can hear my name
                         but that's

            Yonni

                                        how… not sounds.

And it takes my thoughts and my mind.
And it's all I can think about.

You.

You're all I can think about.
You.
Lying there in the road.
You.
A whole year a whole year a whole year ago.
The bike crushed against the – you… the the the wheel of the
truck.
You.

A year a year a year a year

It's all I can think about…
You
All I can think about.
You.
What I did
All I can think about.
To you.

I last precisely fourteen minutes at your funeral.
I can't face your Shiva.

I send Gabby flowers.
Apologise. Hope she can understand.

And I sit in silence.
Staring at the walls for what seems like hours.
We have really shitty wallpaper.
My parents have like zero taste.

And I don't even clock Reuben in the room.
I have no idea why he's here.
NoideaIjustthinkaboutyou.
Or how long he's been watching.

I'm vaguely aware of the *C'mon son.*
Vaguely with it as he takes me up to my room.
Ijustthinkaboutyou.
Cling to him as he tells me to let go. That it's okay to let go.

Ijustthinkaboutyou.

So I let go.
You.
And sob into him.
You.
Into dickhead Reuben like I've never sobbed
You.
And he holds me tight.

And I stand over Dough, wanting to kick the fucking shit out of
him. Wanting to smash in that fat anti-Semitic motherfucker's
face until there's nothing left of it as pain and shame burn red-
hot rivers of tears down my face...

Wanting to –

No no no no no no no...

That doesn't happen.

That doesn't.
You.
I have to see you.

I have to.

Run.

Out into space.
Us two little extra-terrestrials on either side of the solar
system...

Run.

Me. Ganymede.
The largest moon of Jupiter and the solar system, and the only
moon known to have a magnetosphere.

The seventh satellite and third Galilean moon outward from
Jupiter.

Completing an orbit in roughly seven days, Ganymede shares a
one-two-four orbital resonance with Europa and Io.

A million kilometres from Jupiter.

And run

Venus has no natural satellite.
Run.
And orbits the sun.

Alone.

At 108,000,000 km.

I could orbit you... There's enough room.

I hear them behind me and with each yell as they gain ground to
remind me what a dirty little Jew bitch I am.
Ijustthinkaboutyou.

About. About, about about... Orbiting you.
Like.
ET phone home.

And as as as as my heart beats in my mouth beats lungs beat in
my throat beats adrenalin 'cross my chest and tension in my arms
that shivers down my back as legs turn to jelly I realise I need to
think about how I'm going to explain this actually at home...

But later.

Because I have to get to you.
I have to talk to you.
I have to be with you and as I run at the wall of the cemetery
I'm convinced I can clear it.

And it doesn't take long to find you.

And as I curl down next to you memories and calls and chats
and joints and texts and tweets and love and mushrooms and
sex and cider and Sophie and Hebrew and politics and food and
crusades and pics and wine and fun and and movies and and
and some of it real and some of it –

Stop.

The timing of the stone-setting.

Stop.

Can vary from community to community. In Israel, it's usually
at the end of the first month, but here… in Britain we do it at
the end of the year, to coincide with the first –

First anni–

I'm sorry I couldn't come today.

In.

In in in in the Ashkenazi tradition the stone. The stone is left
upright at the head of the grave, but the Sephardim –
We lay them horizontally.

I rest my head against the newly laid headstone. And I tell you
that I never washed your T-shirt.

I don't know why that occurs to me.

The one I slept in the first time I ever stayed over.

That I've had it more than a year. That I stole it from your
bedroom.

That I sleep in it every night.

And I swear it stinks.

But it stinks of you and it stinks of me because it stinks of us and I don't want to stop talking because I'm scared if I do the conversation will be over this time so I want to keep talking so it's like we're in bed and you're waiting patiently for me to finish because you don't want to interrupt but I want to tell you everything so much that I can't stop until I actually tell you everything but there's so much stuff to tell you now because it feels like I haven't seen you for so long and that I don't even know where to start.

But off. In the distance. I hear them again.

Fucking losers.

And I stand.

And I see them.

In triplicate.
A trichotomy.

Heading straight at me.

And I don't want them to see me.
I don't want them to find us.
I don't want them to see me.

And I don't want to fight.
All I've done since I lost you is fight.

I just don't have the energy.
Not any more.

So I run.

Try to avoid them as they gain as they gain.

Run.

Run through graves and memorial, memories and pain

Run.
Through anguish, loneliness, laughter, loss.

Run.

Run run run at the cemetery wall.

But this time run I don't quite make it...

Run.

This time I don't clear the wall…

Just run.

I lose my footing.

Run.
I fall.
And run.
I fall.

With such sheer force that I hurtle through space.

Fall

Past a hundred million tiny stars.

Fall.
Past Venus.

Fall.

And Jupiter.

Fall.

In their serene, expansive, orbital dance

Since the start of this month, Jupiter and and and all the stars
behind it have gradually slipped lower and lower and lower into
the evening twilight.

Whilst Venus hangs high.

I run.
Fall.
Run.

I fall.
Run.
Fall.

Into my orbital dance with you.

As the two brightest planets in the sky shift and circle as they come close, the Goddess of Love and the God of Thunder conjunct to form a luminous double star that lights up the night sky.

Run.

Merging as one, to the left of the moon.

Umismali Gavri'el …

And as they do.

Must run.

I notice how… how flawless Venus' orbit is.

With an eccentricity of less than nought-point-nought-one, an almost perfect circle.

The End.

www.nickhernbooks.co.uk

facebook.com/nickhernbooks

twitter.com/nickhernbooks